TRUTH OR DARE

living by truth in a world that dares you not to

tatum smith

truth or dare

All Rights Reserved ©2018 Tatum Smith. First Printing: 2018. No portion of this book may be copied, retransmitted, reposted, duplicated, or otherwise used without the express written approval of the author, except by reviewers who may quote brief excerpts in connection with a review.

United States laws and regulations are public domain and not subject to copyright. Any unauthorized copying, reproduction, translation, or distribution of any part of this material without permission by the author is prohibited and against the law.

Scripture quotations are taken from THE HOLY BIBLE, NEW INTERNATIONAL VERSION®, NIV® Copyright © 1973, 1978, 1984, 2011 by Biblica, Inc.® Used by permission. All rights reserved worldwide.

Copyright © 2018 Tatum Smith

All rights reserved.

ISBN-10: 1984012649
ISBN-13: 978-1984012647

truth or dare

To Ainsley, Anna, Avery, Bailey, Caitlin, Caroline, Ellis, Grace,
Kailey, Karis, Mary Mac & Molly

truth or dare

contents

a note   i

1   *identity*...5
        confidence...6
        staying in the word...8
        fact over feeling...10
        body image...12
        wearing makeup...14
        perfectionism...16
        working hard...18
        commitment...21

2   *friendship*...23
        the purpose of friendship...24
        friendships with nonbelievers...26
        shifting friendships...29
        fighting with friends...31
        exclusion...33

3   *social media*...37
        examining social media...38
        the power of notifications...40
        social media evaluation...41

4   *family*...45
        parents...46
        siblings...49
        a christ-centered family...51
        serving your family...53
        broken families...56

5 *dating*...59
  godly dating...60
  boundaries...63
  the godly girlfriend...67
  modesty...69
  dating accountability list...71
  dear future husband...73
6 *interactions*...75
  the power of words...76
  minimizing conflict...78
  the judgmental stereotype...80
  loving your enemies...83
7 *digging deep*...85
  drinking...86
  partying...88
  cussing...91
  eating disorders...93
  stress...96
  doubt...98
8 *discipleship*...103
  accountability...104
  mentorships...106
  scripture memory...108
  multiplication...111

truth or dare

a note

To my sister in Christ:

I wrote this little book to share biblical responses to issues you are bound to encounter in one way or another in these next few years. As an 18-year-old student, I understand much of your hardship and have experienced the troubles and confusions discussed in this book. Having applied personal experiences and what I have learned from mentorships and leading other teenagers, I truly believe *Truth or Dare* holds inspiration, hope, and direction for you.

You will stand much more firm in your teenage years when you learn why you believe what you believe and study what Scripture says about challenges you are likely to face. *Truth or Dare*'s simple and short sections are designed to provide you with to-the-point biblical responses to the pressures of middle school and high school. I encourage you to read every lesson because if you do not struggle with a particular topic now, you might in the future, or you will meet someone who does. I pray my book will encourage you to pursue a life of obedience to the Lord, although I do not want you to *solely* focus on obedience. Christianity may seem like a lot of overwhelming rules until you understand one thing: it is a *relationship* – not just a religion. You must get to know God's character by spending time with Him before you will want to walk in full obedience. Spend time in prayer, listening to worship music, reading Scripture, journaling, and sitting in His presence; just hang out with God. As you lean into Him, obedience will become less burdensome and more natural.

Quite simply, the Bible is truth. It is full of encouragement and guidance applicable to the past, present, and future. Truth is constant; unlike everything else in this world, it does not change, which is why believers should pursue a life in accordance with it. Its reliability allows Christians to stand firm and have hope in all circumstances. When you live by truth, you glorify the Lord by acknowledging with your thoughts, words, or actions that He deserves praise. You give Him glory by living out your belief that what He says is worthy of reverence.

In some situations, however, abiding by truth is not always fun, and you will be tempted to manipulate or disregard it. People around you will likely encourage you to neglect it; they will dare you to turn your back on truth. Despite its consistent and unchanging wisdom, you might want to pick and choose which elements of the Word you claim as truth when in reality, it is *all* truth. You do not get to select certain elements of truth to follow and other elements to ignore. You are not the author of truth, so you do not have the authority to make it flexible. You must learn it and honor it – not rewrite it.

While I see the benefits of writing this in high school, I acknowledge that I still have room to grow. I stand firm in the guidance I have written, although I recognize certain interpretations may shift over time.

I hope you find encouragement in *Truth or Dare* and make it your own. My intention is that you will highlight, annotate, and mark all over this book. I challenge you to personalize it and reflect back on your notes and highlights when needed – maybe even share what you learn with others.

Enjoy the following pages. May they prayerfully provide guidance for you in the trials of middle school, high school, college, and beyond.

In Him,
Tatum

tatum smith

chapter one
IDENTITY

confidence

When you are not confident, it is easy to make bad choices. In order to stand firm in your faith, you must know and be confident in the person God has created you to be, which starts with understanding that He makes you brand new. **Second Corinthians 5:17 says, "Therefore, if anyone is in Christ, the new creation has come: The old has gone, the new is here!"** This means no sin will ever define you again because Jesus is making you new every moment. Every past sin and shame is gone – distant from your identity. Each morning, realize God gives you grace and washes off your sins; no mistake can stain who you are. When you let your past define you and fail to recognize your daily fresh start, you will fall into a repetition of sin and convince yourself there is no improving, which is far from the truth. God has made and is still making you new, and this fact should encourage you to live to glorify Him. He made you clean from sin, so do your best to live as sin-free as possible.

Every element of the Lord's creation is awesome and impressive – especially you. Read **Psalm 139:13-18**. He knit you together without a fault. God is perfect, meaning His creations are perfect, and He did not mess up when He made you. He knows your strengths and weaknesses, your talents and passions, and your personality and heart. He made all of those things, and He designed you in such a way that who you are is exactly what He needs to expand His Kingdom. Every component of your being, whether you like it or not, is designed to bring the Lord glory in some form or another, and that sounds pretty awesome to me. He will use your weaknesses to reveal His provision, and what you view as imperfect, He views as a masterpiece. Look around at creation the next time you are outside. God formed the sky, sea, plants, and animals, and He called all of that good in Genesis. What a lot of girls do not realize, however, is that when He created people, He called them *very* good. Do not sell yourself short. Everything about you is a beautiful work of art, so live like it. Treat your body and mind with respect, knowing you are a canvas for God's love and grace.

The Lord made every single person who has ever lived in a specific way, so be okay with being unique. Everyone has different gifts, talents, and personalities, and if you let Him, God will use your originality for His Kingdom. Read **1 Corinthians 12:12-27**. In this passage, Paul uses an analogy of the human body to describe how God made His people. If all you had on your body was eyes, you would not be able to do anything but see. Similarly, if the Lord created everyone with the same gift, His creation would be lacking thousands of other useful gifts. Wherever your talents lie, God can use you and your abilities for His Kingdom. This means you should not compare your qualities to those of other people. The Lord does not value anyone's personality or traits over another; He sees all as His beautiful creation, so embrace who you are. Do not ever talk yourself down or think someone else is better than you because you are exactly who God wants you to be.

Be confident in the new, awesome, and unique person God has crafted you to be, and let your identity in Christ be motivation to glorify Him. Be secure in who you are: a creation of the ultimate Creator.

further encouragement:
Ephesians 2:10 ▲ *Romans 6:1-14* ▲ *Genesis 1:26-27*
Galatians 2:20 ▲ *Colossians 1:16-17* ▲ *Proverbs 31:25*

▲▼▲▼▲▼▲▼▲▼▲▼▲▼▲▼▲▼▲▼▲▼▲▼▲▼▲▼▲▼▲▼

staying in the word

As a follower of Jesus, it is critical you read the Bible daily. This not only strengthens your relationship with Jesus, but it also reminds you of your identity in Him. The Bible is the most important book in the entire world because it is the only direct and physically evident communication you have from Heaven, so you should strive to read it every day.

You do not have to read it for hours each day; a realistic goal is to read for ten minutes each time you open your Bible. I suggest bookending your day with Scripture, which means to read it in the morning and at night. While you might not want to wake up earlier to read the Bible, just remember you might wake up earlier to straighten your hair or to put on makeup – and the Bible is drastically more important. In addition, do not wait until too late at night to get in the Word, or you will be too sleepy. Try reading it every night after you shower or eat dinner.

It can be confusing to know where to start when reading the Bible. I encourage you to start with a New Testament book such as James or Philippians. To stay attentive, it helps if you highlight and make notes in the margins, which are also nice to refer back to when needed. A strategy I often use is to read a passage (really read it; pay attention) and ask and answer these two questions: What does this say about God, and what does this mean for my life? Some people like to write down the answers to these questions in a journal.

You might not want to say it, but everyone knows it is true: reading the Bible can be boring and confusing. However, through boredom and confusion, you can learn more about the Lord. It takes discipline to read His Word daily, but through prayer and expectancy, reading the Bible can become intimate time with the Lord rather than just skimming a page. Pray each time before your read Scripture, and expect to learn something from God. Once you do this, you will become fascinated by Scripture; as you lean into the Word, it becomes more interesting to you.

Confusion is often a really beneficial feeling when reading the Bible because it encourages you to find answers. Make a list of all the questions you have (whether they are about who people, where places are, or the character of God), and spend time finding out the answers by asking others or researching online. To prevent confusion, read about the context of the Scripture you are diving into. For instance, if you are about to start reading Ephesians, search online or ask a friend about its historical context. This will give you a better idea of what is happening in the book and why it was written.

When you read the Bible daily, you have a constant reminder of God's character and your identity in Him. Staying in the Word quiets Satan's lies about your life and reminds you that your true self is only found in the Lord. **2 Timothy 3:16-**

17 says, "All Scripture is God-breathed and is useful for teaching, rebuking, correcting and training in righteousness, so that the servant of God may be thoroughly equipped for every good work." Scripture will never fail you because it is truly words from above; it will sharpen your faith, deepen your wisdom, and prepare you to shine for Jesus. Make a goal to read the Bible daily so you will consistently be reminded of how awesome God is and how awesome He made you.

further encouragement:
Psalm 119:105 ▲ Joshua 1:8 ▲ Matthew 4:4 ▲ Romans 15:4
Hebrews 4:12 ▲ Psalm 119:10-11 ▲ John 1:1

▲▼▲▼▲▼▲▼▲▼▲▼▲▼▲▼▲▼▲▼▲▼▲▼▲▼▲▼▲▼▲▼▲▼▲▼

fact over feeling

Emotions are crazy and constantly changing, especially in teenage years. While it is tempting to let how you feel dominate how you live, this is not at all what you are called to do.

Read **Matthew 7:24-29** from Jesus's Sermon on the Mount. This parable is about foundations. Jesus says if you build your foundation on something other than the Word, your house will easily fall. On the other hand, if you do build it on His Word, nothing can knock your house down. The house in this parable represents your life, and the foundation is what your life is based upon. I love this passage because it reminds me that emotions are an incredibly weak foundation. When you put all your faith in how you feel in a given moment, you will always fall down. If you give into your sad, angry, or overdramatic feelings, it affects your words, actions, and thoughts. It distracts you from Jesus and the way He wants you to live, and you begin to selfishly focus on yourself. When this happens, it is super easy to feel down and mad almost every day, letting your circumstances dictate how you act.

Jesus says that a person who follows His Word will not fall. The Word tells you to put your hope in the Lord over and over again. Never once does it say to put your hope in emotions. Never. The Bible enables you to stand firm in hard times and gives you consistent hope and purpose on bad days. Contrarily, emotions are constantly changing, even within seconds. God is the same always, and emotions are the same rarely. That being said, His Word is a much more stable foundation than emotions.

Your first reaction as a girl is likely to give into your feelings, and it takes lots of discipline to change that. It looks like this: in a moment of emotional overload, remind yourself that what you feel can mean very little; it is what the Bible says (not your feelings) that matters. It sometimes means literally saying to yourself, "What I feel is temporary. What God says is constant." Do not give your emotions the power they beg for. Sometimes you just need to remind yourself that you should try to control your emotions – not let them control you. This does not mean you will immediately stop feeling sad or angry, but it does mean how you feel will not negatively affect how you live. In sadness, read what the Bible says about joy in the Lord. In weakness, read about His strength within you. In anger, read about patience and grace, and in failure, read about God making you new. Memorize the verses you read so your mind will (eventually) automatically come to them during emotional distress.

I am not saying your emotions are invalid or unimportant, and I am not trying to discredit what you feel. It is definitely necessary at times to voice your feelings; to ensure honest and sturdy relationships, your friends, family, and mentors need to know what is happening in your life. Tell your loved ones what you are going through, whether it is good or bad. I am ultimately saying that your actions and words should glorify the Lord regardless of how you feel at a given moment. Emotions can be important, but you should not let them pull you away from how Jesus calls you to live. Anger, sadness, confusion, pride, and joy do not justify sin.

In time, God will reward you for putting your faith in Him over your emotions. The Bible is factual, unlike your shifting feelings. Live fact over feeling.

further encouragement:
1 John 3:20 ▲ Jeremiah 17:9 ▲ Psalm 78:35
Proverbs 15:18 ▲ Romans 12:2 ▲ Romans 8:28

▲▼▲▼▲▼▲▼▲▼▲▼▲▼▲▼▲▼▲▼▲▼▲▼▲▼▲▼▲▼▲▼▲▼

body image

Pop culture taunts girls with the idea of a "perfect body." From magazine covers to Gigi Hadid's Instagram page, girls compare their bodies to stick figure supermodels and bash their builds. But here are some truths I want you to remember:

Genesis 1:27 says, "So God created mankind in His own image, in the image of God He created them; male and female

He created them." In all honesty, you have absolutely no right to criticize your own body. God made you in His holy and divine image, so who are you to question Him? My friend Ashley once told me, "God created all the beautiful constellations in the sky, and we don't sit around and nitpick those. So why would we nitpick ourselves? The stars are not even made in God's image, and we are." Her brilliant words have stuck with me ever since. Do not forget, out of all of God's beautiful creations, literally none of them except humans were created in His image – so it is truthfully not okay to hate on your image, the image of God.

Nowhere in the Bible does it say tummy rolls are sinful or that you must be a certain height to be beautiful. It never says diets are crucial to living a good life or that you should weigh yourself every day, and it does not say blonde is best or that starving yourself is a good idea. God values every part of you, regardless of what society says you should look like.

All girls struggle with body image, including me. If God made us so beautifully, it can be confusing to understand why we still do not like our bodies. I believe Satan puts bad thoughts into our heads about our appearances, whispering that we are not good enough. However, God uses this evil to bring us closer to Him; we must spend time with God to remember our true beauty and worth. He takes the lies of the world and uses them to bring us near to Him.

I am sure you have heard this before, but the Bible says you are wonderfully made. Read **Psalm 139:13-18** aloud. **Psalm 139:14 says, "I praise you because I am fearfully and wonderfully made; Your works are wonderful, I know that full**

well." Here is your challenge: know it full well. That means to truly know it and believe it. It is easy to hear that you are made wonderfully – but to know it is a whole new challenge. It is a process, for sure. Begin by praying about it every single day, asking God to remind you that you are perfect in His image. The more you pray about it, the more you will believe it, and I am speaking from personal experience. Secondly, memorize **Psalm 139:14**, and repeat it to yourself whenever you feel like criticizing your build. Try writing the verse on your mirror with a dry erase marker to serve as a constant reminder. Lastly, have discipline, and do not spend time engaging in activities that cause you to compare your body to others. This could include spending time on social media, watching certain TV shows and movies, or listening to certain music.

You are beautifully made in the image of God. Know it full well.

further encouragement:
1 Peter 3:3-4 ▲ *1 Samuel 16:7* ▲ *Proverbs 31:25*
Proverbs 31:10 ▲ *Proverbs 31:30* ▲ *Genesis 1:27*

▲▼▲▼▲▼▲▼▲▼▲▼▲▼▲▼▲▼▲▼▲▼▲▼▲▼▲▼▲▼

wearing makeup

Wearing makeup is not a sin, but faith in makeup is. Today's culture encourages makeup for certain events such as weddings, church, and graduations, that is totally okay because it is a form of reverence and formality. However, makeup becomes an issue when you rely on it to feel good about yourself. If makeup becomes something you cannot live without, you are insulting the One who created your beautiful face exactly as He wanted it. The Bible says in **Philippians 4:19** that God will meet your every need, meaning you should place dependence only upon Him – not even a little upon makeup. **Psalm 23:1** also supports this idea by saying you lack nothing because of the Lord. *Nothing*. With Him, you have inner and outer beauty, and that is not contingent on wearing makeup.

Starting in eighth grade, I used to wear makeup every day to school. I did not really think much of it; it was just a habit, and most of my friends wore it daily as well. It was the norm for me, and it stayed that way through ninth grade. I carried this daily makeup routine to summer camp, but I felt a little odd when I realized most of the girls around me did not wear makeup. Near the beginning of my term, my counselors covered up the mirrors with trash bags so my cabin mates and I could not see ourselves. It stayed like that for three days, which meant three days of no mascara, bronzer, or concealer, so I had no option other than to walk around camp barefaced. After three days passed, I went to the mirror to do my makeup, and a friend of mine pointed out that if I could go three days without makeup, I could go the rest of the term without it. At the time I felt a little judged, but I did not want to make a fuss so I stowed my makeup bag for the rest of the two weeks, and that proved a turning point for me. The girls around me poured encouragement into me daily, and I read Scripture on my identity in Christ, and all the sudden, going without makeup did not seem so bad anymore. From that summer on, I only wear makeup when necessary, and in all honesty, it is one of the most freeing things I have ever done. Not to mention…going without makeup means sleeping in later in the mornings and not having to worry about rubbing your eyes!

If you find yourself reliant on makeup, maybe giving up it up for a short period of time is a good challenge for you. I encourage you to find Bible verses on your beauty in and dependence upon Christ and pick one or two to write on your bathroom mirror. This will serve as a reminder that you do not need makeup to be beautiful; all you need is Jesus.

further encouragement:
1 Timothy 2:9-10 ▲ *1 Peter 3:3-4* ▲ *1 John 2:16*
Matthew 6:25-34 ▲ *Romans 12:2* ▲ *2 Corinthians 12:9*

▲▼▲▼▲▼▲▼▲▼▲▼▲▼▲▼▲▼▲▼▲▼▲▼▲▼▲▼▲▼▲▼

perfectionism

If you are anything like me, you put a tremendous amount of pressure on yourself to do everything perfectly. From your detailed daily planner to your intricate to-do list to your 4.0 GPA, everything has a place, and everything must be accomplished. This mindset is nice when I am caught up on all I need to do. Most of the time, however, my life is honestly a mess, and I am always super behind on what I need to get done. I make a B on a test or I forget to go to an appointment, and it is the end of the world. Well, it is in the moment of course.

Perfectionism is the thief of allowing God to work through your imperfections. When you want everything to go exactly as planned, that is you wanting to take everything into your own hands and show the world you can thrive without any help. Perfectionism sounds nice, but it is a trap, and it is exhausting. It places a weight on your shoulders, whispering that you have to be your own god, that you have to hide weaknesses and show absolute excellence all the time. If you slip up once or accidentally reveal a fault, it feels as if you will never be viewed as outstanding again. Suddenly, when you show a flaw, you feel weak, lacking, and not good enough. As a Christian, though, you obviously know you are not God, so why do you still put the pressure of perfectionism on yourself?

By trying to hide your weaknesses, you are stealing God's opportunity to shine through them. In **2 Corinthians 12:9-10** Paul says, **"But he said to me, 'For my grace is sufficient for you, for my power is made perfect in weakness.' Therefore I will boast all the more gladly about my weaknesses, so that Christ's power may rest on me. That is why, for Christ's sake, I delight in weakness, in insults, in hardships, in persecutions, in difficulties. For when I am weak, then I am strong."** It says plainly right there that God uses your weaknesses to show His power. That means you should hand Him your imperfections, admit that you are not perfect, and ask Him to weave His glory through your faults. It also says you should take pride in your weaknesses. Not in a way where you go around chanting about your bad grade in algebra, but in a way where you acknowledge that you have an awesome Savior who takes your imperfections and transforms them into His strength. What incredible news this is! When you are weak, no matter the situation, if you prayerfully hand it over to God, He will eventually use it for His Kingdom.

God does this in a number of ways, and sometimes you

might not even realize it. For instance, He might use your shortcomings to teach you a lesson or to draw you closer to Him, to make you more reliant on Him and less reliant on yourself. He might even use your weaknesses to benefit others. This could come through conversations reflecting **2 Corinthians 12:9-10**, or it could be through people watching you handle your weaknesses as a place for God's provision. Nonetheless, embrace your imperfections, because they are no longer flaws, but Heavenly strength. Perfectionism has no grip on you.

further encouragement:
1 John 1:8 ▲ Ecclesiastes 7:20 ▲ Romans 8 ▲ 2 Samuel 22:31
Hebrews 10:14 ▲ Ephesians 2:8-9 ▲ Romans 3:23

▲▼▲▼▲▼▲▼▲▼▲▼▲▼▲▼▲▼▲▼▲▼▲▼▲▼▲▼▲▼

working hard

Contrary to perfectionism, some girls struggle with work ethic. It is tiring to give 100% effort in everything you do, especially when you are trying to juggle academics, athletics, religion, a job, and spending time with loved ones. It is easy to slack off a little bit, such as settling for a zero on your homework or showing up late. Sometimes you think you can get by if you just give 60% in each area of your life; you convince yourself it is okay if you do not give full effort – as long as you accomplish a given task. You lower your standards of diligence, especially during busy and stressful seasons.

Unlike your probable tendencies, **Colossians 3:23** says, **"Whatever you do, work at it with all your heart, as working for the Lord, not for human masters."** Although this verse was directed toward servants, it can certainly be applied to you – a servant of God. Working at something with all your heart does not mean just getting by or going through the motions; it means giving every single ounce of effort you have to offer. This becomes extremely difficult when you view humans as your audience. Your mom might be okay with a B if she thinks you are trying your hardest because she does not know your intentions. If you are sweating in practice, your coach might think you are giving your best, even if you are cutting corners when no one is watching. On the other hand, God knows your heart and recognizes when you just give half effort, so He should be your true audience.

Your motivation to give full effort should be that the Lord gave you the ability to give full effort in whatever environment you find yourself. For instance, if you are on a sports team, God has blessed you with an able body and the ability to compete. He placed you in your school for a reason, knowing it would be a great environment for you to shine His light. God smiles when you do your best, and it brings Him praise when you use the abilities He gave you to full potential.

Your schedule might be a little too crazy for you to give solid effort in everything. If this is the case, you probably need to clean some activities off your plate. If you want to truly and fully glorify the Lord in all your activities, design a schedule where that is possible. Your goal should not be to impress people with your packed calendar; rather, it should be to give your all in everything you do, even if it means doing less.

Colossians 3:23 also means you are supposed to work at growing in your spiritual life with your whole heart. In fact, this should be your number one priority. If you do not have time in your schedule to spend with God, either wake up earlier or commit to less. Period. You must have quality time with the Lord by praying, reading Scripture, and resting in His presence. Likewise, you should make time to be involved in your church. God will reveal opportunities to you, and the level of commitment He wants you to have in the church will become apparent. Make sure you follow His lead, whether that is joining or leading a small group, going to weekly worship nights, or volunteering. Give your all in growing spiritually, even if it means committing to less. Full effort in your spiritual life comes first no matter what.

Galatians 6:9 encourages Believers to keep doing good, so do not tire of being productive for the Kingdom. Remember that the Lord is your strength, and He will equip and empower you to accomplish tasks that appear daunting. You are responsible for effective time management, but God will assist you where you ask for His help. Give your all in all you do. God knows your heart, and He knows when you are giving full effort. He does not expect you to be absolutely perfect in all your activities, but He does expect you to give your best.

further encouragement:
Proverbs 13:4 ▲ *Matthew 6:33* ▲ *Colossians 3:17*
Acts 2:42-47 ▲ *Proverbs 14:23* ▲ *1 Corinthians 10:31*

▲▼▲▼▲▼▲▼▲▼▲▼▲▼▲▼▲▼▲▼▲▼▲▼▲▼▲▼▲▼

commitment

Commitment is not something that usually comes to mind when thinking about Jesus. It is quite underrated in whatever form it takes – whether it is having a "change of plans" or being lazy. However, commitment is a big deal to God, so it should be a big deal to you.

There is no debate about the Lord's commitment to you. He is there for you all the time, even when it does not feel like it. He always shows up, and He invests in every second of your life, which is evident all throughout Scripture. Since God is dedicated to you, you should be dedicated to Him in return, and it looks like this: reading your Bible daily, walking in obedience, maintaining a solid prayer life, and shining His light. Basically, God's commitment to you is that He loves you all the time, so your commitment to Him is that you will love Him back all the time. **1 John 4:19 says, "We love because he first loved us."** Love Him with your time, actions, words, and thoughts.

After your commitment to God comes your commitment to the people you love, which means making time for loved ones. Maybe for you, it means actually talking to your dad when he gets home from work, spending time with your little sister, or hanging out with your friend who has been having a hard week. There are no excuses for not making time for loved ones. God calls you to love everyone, and commitment and love go hand in hand. Being committed to loved ones also means being devoted to praying for them, showing them more of Jesus, and not letting feelings affect your relationships. It is easy to let a fight ruin things, but if a relationship is rooted in Jesus, stay loyal to it and look beyond the argument.

On a super practical level, stay committed to the plans you make. FOMO, or fear of missing out, often keeps people from sticking to plans. Everyone has felt it. Imagine this: a friend asks you to spend the night, and you say yes, but another friend (whom you would rather be with) asks you to hang out as well. What do you do? Countless girls have been in this situation before, and whether or not you have given into changing your plans, you have definitely been tempted to do so. But is ditching original plans to hang out with someone else an act of love? Nope – and it is definitely not an act of commitment. When you commit to a person, there should be no question about whether or not you will come through. Be reliable. Be consistent. Be the girl who sticks to her word, even if it takes a little sacrifice.

God's commitment to you means you must be dedicated to Him and to His people. Do not underestimate the power of commitment.

further encouragement:
Galatians 6:9 ▲ *Acts 2:42-47* ▲ *Mark 12:30-31*
1 Corinthians 13 ▲ *1 Kings 8:61* ▲ *Romans 12:2* ▲ *Luke 9:23*

▲▼▲▼▲▼▲▼▲▼▲▼▲▼▲▼▲▼▲▼▲▼▲▼▲▼▲▼▲▼▲▼▲▼

chapter two
FRIENDSHIP

the purpose of friendship

The purpose of friendship in today's world is cloudy and usually forgotten. You make friends because it is what you were raised to do, and there is nothing in the world wrong with that. Believers often forget, however, why friendships exist. They do not simply exist to exist. Like He did with everything else in creation, the Lord created friendship to glorify Him. True friends are gifts intended to give Him praise and honor in a number of ways. Real friends are those who encourage you, in whatever form that takes, and they are the people who value you as a sister in Christ and remind you of your worth in Him. They pray for you and listen to you and care about you. Ultimately, a true friend motivates you to grow closer to Jesus, and you do the same for her. This is the purpose of friendship, as it brings God glory.

Proverbs 27:17 says, **"As iron sharpens iron, so one person sharpens another."** Two people who are friends are meant to sharpen and improve one another. Iron physically sharpens iron, so the two make each other better. *Find friends who are iron!* Your friendships should inspire ingenuity, strengthen judgment, and motivate righteousness. Hang out with girls who will encourage you to go to church, student ministries, or Bible studies. For example, on a mission trip during my freshman year of high school, I became good friends with four peers from another school. These friends sharpened me in a way for which I am forever grateful: they introduced me to my church's weekly student ministry, Echo. I found that Echo consistently provided enlightening sermons, brought me closer to the Lord through worship, and allowed me to meet even more iron friends. I am still close with the four friends who first invited me to Echo, and I am so grateful they strengthened my church involvement.

There are other ways friends can be iron as well. They might share Scripture with you, hold you accountable for your actions, or simply have honest and intentional conversations with you. Iron friends will encourage you to work hard in all your activities. They will help you hug your morals, they will give advice, and they will provide listening ears. When this happens, your friendships will be unique, deep, and genuine; friends centered on Jesus get to bond and grow in a special way that nonbelievers will never get to experience. I challenge you to befriend people who are going to spur you closer to Christ as you do the same for them.

Nonetheless, I want to acknowledge that no one is perfect (**Romans 3:23**), so you cannot expect your friends to be perfect all the time. Friends will let you down. They will forget to respond to your texts, they will slack on a commitment, and they might even say something hurtful. This does not mean these people are not your true friends. You are not perfect, and you might accidentally do the same things to them. All in all, regardless of the small and infrequent slip-ups, if the friendship brings you and your friend closer to Jesus, it is worth it – even when things get tough.

Take a second and think about a few of your closest friends. It is likely you are somewhat of a combination of those few people since good friends generally share similar morals, hobbies, and beliefs. Consider whether or not these are the type of people you want to be like. I encourage you to be honest with yourself and pray God reveals to you which friendships glorify Him and which do not.

further encouragement:
1 Thessalonians 5:11 ▲ *1 Corinthians 15:33* ▲ *Romans 1:11-12*
Proverbs 13:20 ▲ *Colossians 3:12-14* ▲ *Ecclesiastes 4:9-10*
Proverbs 12:26

▲▼▲▼▲▼▲▼▲▼▲▼▲▼▲▼▲▼▲▼▲▼▲▼▲▼▲▼▲▼

friendships with nonbelievers

Your closest and best friends should be people who bring you closer to Jesus as you simultaneously bring them closer to Jesus. If someone lacks a real relationship with the Lord, she is not the person to be very best friends with because she does not share your perspective on life. However, you can still have a friendship with her, regardless of her religious views.

If a person is loudly sinning, such as drinking, sending inappropriate pictures, or bullying others, do not hang around her all the time. If you do, people will associate you with her and give you a bad reputation, even if you did nothing wrong. As a Christian, people should generally be able to look at you and your friends and see that something is different about you all, that you are good, moral, kind, and uplifting people. When you mostly hang out with intentional and loud sinners, it is hard for others to look at you and see Christ simply because you are associated with people whose lives do not reflect Him.

Do not be best friends with a nonbeliever and justify it with the idea that you are going to convert her to Christianity.

That is in the Holy Spirit's hands; you can show her more of Jesus, but it is not your job to convert her. You must also be aware that sinful actions can influence yours no matter how much you say they will not. If you think her sins will not affect you, **1 Corinthians 15:33** proves you wrong: **"Bad company corrupts good character."** Say your best friend drinks every weekend, but you have promised yourself you will not. Because she is your best friend, she will likely convince you to sip some alcohol at one point or another. Even if it is just a little, it is still a sin (because you are underage), and it could lead to flexibility in your morals. I have seen so many friends lost to drinking, sex, and other tangible sins simply because they spent most of their time with people who indulged in these actions. Even some of my friends who were once strong in their faith fell to alcohol, smoking, or impurity merely because other peers encouraged them to do so. Maintain high standards for your best friends, and stay cautious of people who will encourage you to bend your morals.

However, remember that Jesus did indeed hang out with tax collectors. At His time, tax collectors were dirty and immoral; they were the lowest of the low. Nonetheless, Jesus hung out with them to show them His love and grace. He sought to introduce them to a different type of lifestyle, whether or not they wanted to accept it. He did the same thing with other loud sinners, such as adulterers, liars, and thieves. Friendships with people who do not follow Jesus are awesome because they put you in a position to witness to others, directly or indirectly. These types of friendships sometimes provide opportunities to share the Gospel with someone who has never heard it, which you cannot do if you only hang out with Believers. Other times, you cannot directly talk about Jesus with friends who do not care about Him. In these cases, you can show them His love through encouraging words, listening ears, kind actions, and supportive hearts.

When you strictly limit yourself to one group of friends, even if it is one Godly group, you limit your opportunities to witness to others. If you find friends who love Jesus, it is awesome to spend a lot of time with them – but do not isolate yourself. I am not suggesting that you be best friends with nonbelievers, but I am suggesting that it is okay to occasionally sit with them at lunch. You can talk to them between classes and maybe even grab ice cream with them after school. It is fine to mix up whom you hang out with because that gives you opportunities to show more people the light of Christ. As long as you are wary of association and cautious of ungodly company, being surface level friends with nonbelievers will not hurt you.

Nevertheless, you must remember to stay on guard. You can easily slip away from the Lord without noticing when you surround yourself with people who do not follow Him. Even if you only spend a small portion of time with nonbelievers, stay cautious of your actions, decisions, and words. Jesus hung out with intentional sinners, but not *all* the time. You should dedicate more of your time to friends who follow Him because you cannot provide all the spiritual encouragement and accountability you need, and you cannot always listen to and inspire yourself. That is what Jesus-centered friendships are for. More than any other peers, hang out with friends who bring you closer to Jesus. While you can have friendships with nonbelievers, your best friends should be girls rooted in the Lord.

further encouragement:
Proverbs 13:20 ▲ *Proverbs 18:24* ▲ *Proverbs 22:24-25*
Proverbs 27:17 ▲ *Proverbs 12:26* ▲ *Mark 2:13-17*

▲▼▲▼▲▼▲▼▲▼▲▼▲▼▲▼▲▼▲▼▲▼▲▼▲▼▲▼▲▼

shifting friendships

Having friends is not something you are promised in your Christian faith. When you give Jesus everything, you truly give Him everything, including the right to leave you friendless. However, I personally believe if you pray for friends who will lead you closer to the Lord, He will eventually provide. Maybe not immediately, but He will provide. God wants to give you friendships that will glorify Him, so you just have to trust His timing and walk in obedience.

If you are transitioning away from ungodly friends, there is a good chance you will temporarily lack a core group of friends. That can be a hard line to walk: living in one season without close Godly friends or settling for spending all your time with friends who pull you away from the Lord. It is definitely tempting to lower your standards of friendship, especially when you are at home alone while everyone else is out drinking. It really stinks – speaking from personal experience.

However, imagine being so strong in your faith that you could say, "God, You are all I need. Be my only friend if You have to be." God could be using your season of loneliness to draw you closer to Him and to prepare your heart for future Godly friendships. Stay strong when you are tempted to become best friends with someone who is not living life with Jesus. God knows what He is doing in your season of loneliness, and He will not abandon you. **Isaiah 55:8-9 says, "'For my thoughts are not your thoughts, neither are your ways my ways,' declares the Lord. 'As the heavens are higher than the earth, so are my ways higher than your ways and my thoughts than your thoughts.'"** You do not get to see His plan from an aerial view, and you are not able to understand His processes. Luckily, the future of your friendships (or the lack of) is in the hands of the King of kings.

Near the beginning of high school, my best friend and I had a falling out. She had been my one close Jesus-following friend at school, and the end of our friendship brought a tough and lonely season for me. After I spent much time praying and waiting for the Lord to pull through, a group of girls from another school walked into my life; once I acknowledged my need for a core group of Christian friends, He did not disappoint. Today, these kind, gentle, and loving girls are my best friends, and they were totally worth the season of waiting.

Remember that people change, and so will friends. That is why it is wrong to put all your hope and trust in humans. Like everything besides the Lord, they are inconsistent, even if they do not mean to be. God is the only One who will remain constant, so put your faith in Him, not friends.

further encouragement:
Romans 3:23 ▲ *Ecclesiastes 3:1*▲ *Psalm 34:17-20*
Philippians 4:19 ▲ *Matthew 28:20* ▲ *Deuteronomy 31:6*

fighting with friends

People are not perfect (**Romans 3:23**), which means friendships are not perfect. It is completely normal to fight with some of your best friends because sin is in the world. In most cases, there is no reason to drop a close friend just because she made one mistake. Unless a close friend physically harmed you, intentionally caused you intense emotional hurt, or stopped bringing you closer to Jesus for a long period of time, do not give up on her so easily. People mess up, and all friendships face difficulties. In all honesty, it is unavoidable. While it is possible to minimize fights, there is no way to completely eliminate them.

Just remember, if a best friend has officially and completely stopped bringing you closer to Jesus, maybe it is time to move on. However, I did not say to end the friendship if she temporarily stopped bringing you closer to Jesus. Keep in mind your friend might be having a tough season of life, and you might have no idea what she is going through. If you suspect this is the case, love on her and stick by her side; be a source of spiritual encouragement for her when she does not have the energy to give you encouragement. Friends love each other in hardships, even though love is not always reciprocated every second. Your friendship does not exist for fun or to make you feel good. It exists to provide mutual encouragement, prayer, and comfort. Have a selfless perspective, and recognize that one of your jobs is to love your iron friend regardless of her shortcomings. Nonetheless, if she begins to pull you away from the Lord, that is when it becomes an issue. Talk with a mentor, and ask God to show you whether it is time to exit that friendship or if your friend just needs some extra love.

Most of the time, fighting with true friends is just a speed bump. It slows you down and maybe even scares you, but it does not last forever. It is important to trust that if the friendship truly glorifies God, He will not punish you for that. If your friend did something to wrong you, ask yourself if you will still be angry at her in a year from now. If the answer is no (it probably is), you have an excellent opportunity to exercise forgiveness, which is accomplished through mental discipline and prayer. Whenever you get angry, remember that everyone messes up, and gear your mind toward grace. Ask the Lord to give you a forgiving heart, and pray for your friendship. **Proverbs 17:17** says, **"A friend loves at all times."** Do not expect your best friend to actively love you literally all the time, because she is not perfect. Neither are you, but you can *try* to love at all times. Active love encourages, apologizes, and prays. It brings forgiveness, compassion, and steadiness. All seasons pass, and if she is a true friend, things will move uphill if you continue to exercise love.

There are plenty of ways to minimize fights. For example, throughout middle school, I noticed friends like to one-up each other – tell a better story, say a funnier joke, or take more attention. Maybe for you, minimizing fights means you must stop trying to one-up your friend. I have endured fights with friends who get upset because I did not listen to them. Turn your listening ears on because that is one of your jobs as a true friend. Remember to exemplify the fruits of the Spirit in your friendships. **Galatians 5:22-23** says these are "**love, joy, peace, forbearance, kindness, goodness, faithfulness, gentleness and self-control.**" Lastly, pray God gives you and your friends the ability to recognize and lay down small and petty fights. Fighting with a friend over why she did not answer your text is not worth the trouble.

Above all, remember that your job as an iron friend is to actively build friendships that glorify Christ. Simply do your job, and the number of fights will decrease.

further encouragement:
Colossians 3:12-14 ▲ *Romans 3:23* ▲ *Luke 6:31*
John 15:12-13 ▲ *1 John 1:8* ▲ *Ecclesiastes 4:9-10*

▲▼▲▼▲▼▲▼▲▼▲▼▲▼▲▼▲▼▲▼▲▼▲▼▲▼▲▼▲▼

exclusion

Being left out is far from uncommon. I am willing to bet every middle school girl has felt left out at one point or another because it is basically unavoidable. Like my peers, I struggled with this in middle school, and to be honest, it does not completely go away in high school. When you are the person who is left out, it is easy to remember every single way your friends have excluded you. It is easy to bash yourself and convince yourself that your friends do not like you or that you are the oddball out.

What it is not easy to do, however, is to consider the likely truth that your friends probably did not mean to leave you out. If you are being realistic, it is highly probable you have accidentally left out a friend. If you do not think you have left someone out, just think about all the times you have hung out with your best friend and did not invite the other girls who sit near you at lunch. Leaving people out is not something commonly done on purpose; the truth is that the person being left out often exaggerates the situation in her head. It sounds harsh, I know. But honestly, with this perspective, your teenage years will be a lot happier. If you can take a step back from the situation and consider that your friends did not intentionally leave you out, you will feel a lot better about yourself.

It is also important to remember that everyone cannot invite everyone to everything. Maybe your friends needed to have a serious conversation, and that is why they are hanging out without you. Maybe their parents organized a time for them to see each other, or maybe they just wanted some quality time. They probably did not actually think "Hm…Should we invite her? Nah!" If these people call you their friend, it is really unlikely they did not invite you because they do not want to spend time with you. You cannot hold your friends to the standard of inviting you to every single thing they do. Just because they wanted quality time with another friend does not mean your friendship is broken.

However, there may be times when girls intentionally exclude you. This might be when they do it over and over again and brag about it to your face. I know that feeling from middle school, and it stinks. Before you determine if someone is purposefully leaving you out, pray about it and talk with a parent or mentor. Luckily, there is a really big realization that sparks from being intentionally left out: those girls are not your real friends! People who exclude you on purpose are not the people you want to surround yourself with. Those are not the girls who are going to have your back during hard times, and those probably are not the girls Jesus has planned for your future friendship path. This can be a difficult realization because it means looking for new friends and exiting your comfort zone, but speaking from personal experience, moving beyond intentionally exclusive friends to seek girls who actually care for you is far worth it.

If you find yourself intentionally leaving other girls out, take a step back from the situation and reconsider. The world is not going to end if you have five girls spend the night instead of four. Consider how you are making others feel by excluding them. I am not saying you must always include everyone because I understand there are times when you just want to hang out with a small group. However, if you are bragging about your dinner plans or posting about your sleepovers to lift yourself up, you are doing something wrong. If you invite all your friends to hang out except one, imagine how the girl left out will feel. You know when you are purposefully leaving someone out, but you also know how it feels to be excluded, so have empathy for others. **1 Corinthians 10:23-24 says, "'I have the right to do anything,' you say – but not everything is beneficial. 'I have the right to do anything'– but not everything is constructive. No one should seek their own good, but the good of others."** No one can truly make you do anything, so it is up to you whether or not you are inclusive of others. However, just because you can make your own choices does not mean every choice you make will be beneficial. Consider how others feel when you leave them out. Have empathy, and put your selfish wants aside, because exclusiveness is not constructive.

further encouragement:
Proverbs 18:2 ▲ *1 Peter 3:8-9* ▲ *Colossians 3:12-14*
Ephesians 4:32 ▲ *Luke 6:31* ▲ *John 13:34-35*

▲▼▲▼▲▼▲▼▲▼▲▼▲▼▲▼▲▼▲▼▲▼▲▼▲▼▲▼▲▼

chapter three
SOCIAL MEDIA

examining social media

Social media is as beneficial or as detrimental as you make it. While it provides ways to spread the Gospel and share what Jesus has done in your life, it also provides paths that may lead you away from the Lord. What you post will affect how people view you, and it will contribute to whether or not people see Jesus reflected in you. Everything on social media is either productive for or destruction to the Gospel. Ranging from captions to comments to photos, social media provides amazing ways to tell people about the great things God is doing in your life, so it is important to recognize this outstanding tool in spreading the Good News. However, this does not mean every single thing you post has to be about Jesus. For example, even a "Happy Birthday" post can show how you lift up and love others, which is glorying to the Lord. Keep in mind that your profile is the first information many people will know about you, so it is really important to make it something that reflects God's love within you. I am not saying your profile must have a Bible verse or Christian quote in it. Those make awesome bios, but any uplifting words will show people you have a special joy in your heart. Remember: as your number of followers increases so does the number of people you have the chance to show the light of Jesus.

Just because social media can be used to share your joy in Christ does not mean it is always beneficial. Lots of times, there are inappropriate advertisements and posts, and even feed that is not obviously inappropriate can distract you from Jesus. For instance, comparing your body to someone's bikini photo is definitely a negative, even though girls do it all the time. Social media makes it easy for you to compare yourself to others, and as a Christian, that is not something you are called to do; you are called to trust that you are made in God's image, which elevates your purpose (**Genesis 1:26-27**). Social media oftentimes fills your mind with lies about yourself and the world, so it is important to follow people and accounts that lift you up and never tear you down.

Checking your feed can waste a lot of your time. For me, once I start scrolling on Instagram, it is hard to make myself stop, and it is likely you are the same way. In these moments, I get wrapped up in comparisons and trends, and I fall distracted from my daily purpose of spreading the love of Jesus. **Psalm 90:12 says, "Teach us to number our days, that we may gain a heart of wisdom."** This verse is a reminder that Believers should make the best use of their time on earth, and this applies to you and me. By taking advantage of the time given to you, you gain wisdom and opportunities to spread the love of the Lord. Coming from someone about to move off to college, I wish I could take back much of the time I spent on social media. Instead of looking through feed, I could have been serving, journaling, or engaging in genuine conversation. Scrolling on social media for hours on end is not the best use of your time: it is simply a waste. Do not throw away your eighteen years at home.

Social media is what you make it. It is up to you whether or not you use it to glorify the Lord, and it is up to you to faithfully manage the time He has given you here on earth.

further encouragement:
Ephesians 5:15-17 ▲ Colossians 4:5 ▲ Romans 12:1-2
John 3:30 ▲ Psalm 115:1 ▲ Philippians 4:8

▲▼▲▼▲▼▲▼▲▼▲▼▲▼▲▼▲▼▲▼▲▼▲▼▲▼▲▼▲▼

the power of notifications

Social media becomes a problem when it hinders you from seeking God. In the last lesson, we established that social media can be used for the Kingdom once you learn to use it in a manner worthy of Christ. However, even if you are using it to lift up Jesus, social media can still be distracting. Apps such as Instagram, Snapchat, and Twitter love to remind you to check your feed and like-count by sending you notifications. It is like Satan whispering in your ear, "Come on, checking social media for five minutes won't hurt," when in reality five minutes can lead to an hour of comparing your profile to others. Satan also uses notifications to say, "Hey, don't forget to look at how many likes you have," as if that really matters. Your worth comes from Jesus, not likes. But even if you understand this, it is still easy to slip into improper use of social media when notifications constantly poke at you.

In **Philippians 4:8**, Paul writes, **"Whatever is true, whatever is noble, whatever is right, whatever is pure, whatever is lovely, whatever is admirable—if anything is excellent or praiseworthy—think about such things."** You are supposed to dwell on truth so you can make your thoughts optimistic and Christ-centered. As innocent as notifications might seem, they can temporarily distract you from what is noble, right, pure, lovely, admirable, and so on. They tempt you to seek value in likes and followers by leading you down a path of constant comparison. One little notification can lead to distraction from thinking about excellent and praiseworthy things.

I challenge you to turn off all your social media notifications. Nearly every social media application or site has the option to turn them off, whether that is through your phone settings or the app itself. My friends and I have done this for years, and it is so freeing. Without notifications, forgetting about social media is easier, and I feel encouraged to use my time for better things than scrolling through my feed. It is a great way to rid yourself of the constant pressure social media places on you, and it better allows you to think about Jesus more than social pressure. Turning off your notifications is a deed well worth it.

further encouragement:
1 Peter 5:8 ▲ 2 Corinthians 11:14 ▲ Proverbs 4:23
Psalm 19:14 ▲ Psalm 119:15 ▲ 1 Corinthians 16:13

social media evaluation

If you are being honest, not every single social media site is beneficial to your walk with Jesus. On the following pages, list the pros and cons of each of your social media apps. Talk about your list with your accountability partner or mentor, and make the decision to delete social media pages that lead you away from Jesus.

I know what you are thinking: you might lose your Snapchat streak. If this is your concern, that is a sign you should take a break from Snapchat. I encourage you to take a step back and consider what true benefit you actually gain from a streak.

Deleting social media seems radical at first, but strengthening your bond with the Lord is much more important than strengthening your bond with your followers. Keep in mind you do not have to delete an account permanently. Try deleting the app off your phone for a couple months until you are certain you can have that page without it distracting you from your identity in Jesus. For the social media pages you choose to keep, list a few goals you have to make them glorify Jesus.

my social media evaluation:

Name of App:

Pros:

Cons:

Goals:

Name of App:

Pros:

Cons:

Goals:

Name of App:

Pros:

Cons:

Goals:

tatum smith

chapter four
FAMILY

parents

Like mine, your relationship with your parents probably varies from season to season or even day to day. There are days when my parents and I get along perfectly fine, and I absolutely love spending time with them, and then there are days when I do not want to talk to them at all; I do not want to answer any questions about my day, and I do not want to hear any lectures. A child/parent relationship is much like the weather in my hometown of Little Rock – unpredictable and constantly changing. No relationship is perfect because no human is perfect (**Romans 3:23**), although it is possible to have a steady, healthy relationship with your parents. In order to have a consistently good relationship, it is important to understand parents' duty toward their child, and a child's duty toward her parents.

The duty of your parents is to love you and to lead you in a manner worthy of Christ. Love comes first, above all. In **John 15:12**, Jesus says to love others the way He loves us, which means parents are to love their children with the same sacrificial and totally unconditional love Jesus gives. Even when their kids screw up or disrespect them, love should be parents' first reaction. Jesus loves you when you do not deserve to be loved, when you do not show Him love, and when you do not make time for Him, so parents should try to imitate this type of love with their children.

Parents should also lead their children in a Christ-like manner. This command is given in **Proverbs 22:6**, which says, **"Start children off on the way they should go; even when they** are old they will not turn from it." This means parents should carefully consider their actions and words, acknowledging that their kids are (often subconsciously) watching their every move. They should think about their attitudes, their work ethic, and their interactions with other adults when setting examples for their children. Everything Christian parents do should ideally point to Christ, and they should raise their kids in their beliefs through reading devotionals as a family, praying together, and going to church.

Because it is their job to lead you, your parents have the right to set guidelines and discipline you. You must also remember your parents set rules because they love you and want to protect you, just as Jesus does for His followers. Respect the guidelines your parents make, and acknowledge their right to discipline you when you deliberately disobey.

As a child, your duty is to love and to follow your parents. Love your parents with the same unconditional love Jesus shows you. You have to love them even when you really do not want to, and you have to love them even when you think they are too strict or when they do something to upset you. This type of love is not accomplished simply through telling your parents you love them before bed. Rather, this unconditional love means loving your parents with your time, actions, and words. You should also practice obedience and respect as avenues to show your love. Your parents are your leaders, and they are hopefully doing the best they can to set an example for you, so be a good follower. Not everything your parents do will be Christ-like; just like you, they are human and will mess up. It is their good and Godly actions you must strive to follow, forgiving their inevitable slip-ups. Pray for the ability to recognize their times of good leadership and mimic those in your own life.

Be super grateful to your parents. Thank them for every meal, new pair of shoes, or vacation – really anything they give you. Children, including me, so easily take for granted what their parents freely provide. You must remember that every dollar your mom and dad spend on you was a dollar they had to earn in the office, so make sure you show your appreciation. They sacrifice their time and money so they can provide for you, so the least you can do is say a quick thank you.

Prayer is crucial to a good child/parent relationship. Pray for your parents to have the strength and ability to actively love you and lead you in Christ, and pray for their specific needs. In the same way, encourage your parents to pray that you will be a good follower of them and that you will continue to grow in the Lord. A great way to encourage this is to ask your parents each night if they have any prayer requests.

I encourage you to reread this section with your parents. Discuss ways to strengthen your relationship with them, and spend time in prayer together. I have no idea what it is like to lead a family, so your parents will probably have much more to say on this topic. I encourage you to talk with them about how you can work together to build a family even more focused on Jesus.

further encouragement:
Exodus 20:12 ▲ Ephesians 6:4 ▲ Isaiah 38:19
1 John 4:19 ▲ Proverbs 6:20-22 ▲ Proverbs 15:20

▲▼▲▼▲▼▲▼▲▼▲▼▲▼▲▼▲▼▲▼▲▼▲▼▲▼▲▼▲▼▲▼▲▼

siblings

Whether you are the oldest, middle, or youngest child, having siblings can be draining and frustrating. If there is one word to describe siblings at young ages, I am tempted to use the word "annoying." My own siblings definitely test my patience each day, and many times I do not respond with gentleness.

It is key to remember that family (including siblings) is a gift from God. Family allows you to grow spiritually at home, keeps you from being lonely, and brings many laughs and smiles. Most of the time, you know your family members will be there for you no matter what happens, and if you do not feel this way with your siblings yet, you probably will someday (I sometimes still have to remind myself of this!). You did nothing to earn a family; God does not owe it to you. So if you have the gift of siblings from the Lord, why do you complain about it? Why is your first response toward your siblings annoyance or frustration? Why don't you actively love them every chance you get and thank Jesus for them?

Siblings will always push your buttons, intentionally and unintentionally, which is merely a result of age differences and living together. It is how you handle the times of annoyance that show your intentions with your sibling relationships. Here is how I try to look at it: I am the oldest sibling, and I only have 18 years at my house. That means 16 years with my younger sister and 13 years with my younger brother. This is likely the only time in my life I will live side-by-side with my siblings, which means it is the only time in my life I will get to love on them and point them to Jesus every single day. This is easy to forget in times of irritation, and I have to consistently remind myself to be intentional with my time with my brother and sister.

Intentionality with your siblings can be expressed in a variety of ways. For instance, pray for your siblings daily and exchange prayer requests with them, even if it is awkward at first. Send them encouraging text messages on big or hard days, and spend quality time with them, even if you never say one word about Jesus the whole time. Focus on building honest and genuine conversation; get past the small talk. Ask them how they are doing, and mean it. Although this takes self-discipline, respond with gentleness and grace in frustrating situations. Maybe even let your sister borrow your clothes when she asks! It will not be the end of the world, I promise. Memorize Scripture with your siblings, even just one or two verses a month. You could go through a book of the Bible or read a short devotional with them each night before bed. The list goes on and on, but it really comes down to actively loving your siblings. This applies to you even if you are not the oldest child; you still have an influence on all your siblings. **1 Timothy 4:12 says, "Don't let anyone look down on you because you are young, but set an example for the Believers in speech, in conduct, in love, in faith, and in purity."** Set an example for your siblings, regardless of your age differences.

1 Corinthians 13:4-7 says, "Love is <u>patient</u>, love is <u>kind</u>. It <u>does not envy</u>, it <u>does not boast</u>, it is <u>not proud</u>. It <u>does not dishonor</u> others, it is <u>not self-seeking</u>, it is <u>not easily angered</u>, it <u>keeps no record of wrongs</u>. Love does not delight in

evil but <u>rejoices with the truth</u>. It always <u>protects</u>, always <u>trusts</u>, always <u>hopes</u>, always <u>perseveres</u>." Write down the underlined words somewhere you will frequently see them, such as on your mirror or in your notebook. Remember **1 Corinthians 13:4-7** in your relationships with your siblings, and pray God will fill your interactions with fruit of the underlined words.

further encouragement:
James 1:19 ▲ *Proverbs 17:17* ▲ *Ephesians 4:32*
Psalm 90:12 ▲ *1 Peter 4:8* ▲ *1 John 4:7*

▲▼▲▼▲▼▲▼▲▼▲▼▲▼▲▼▲▼▲▼▲▼▲▼▲▼▲▼▲▼

a christ-centered family

There is a difference between being a Christian family and being a family built on Christ. Maybe your family goes to church and never talks about Jesus other than on Sunday mornings. But don't worry: if your family is like this, it is an awesome place to start. My challenge for you, though, is to build a family even more centered on the Lord. Here are some super practical ways to build a family where talking about Jesus is the norm:

- Have a short Bible study with your family. Even five to ten minutes of reading Scripture together will help unite your family in Christ. It can be as simple as reading a short devotional or a Psalm each night before bed.
- Memorize Bible verses together. Take turns choosing a Bible verse, hang it on the refrigerator, and take a

couple of weeks to memorize it. Quiz your family on the verse periodically, whether it is in person or by sending a quick text during the day. Hold each other accountable for memorizing it.

- Encourage your family with Scripture. If your mom is having a stressful week, write a comforting Bible verse on a sticky note and put it in her car or on her mirror. If your dad has a long week at work, text him a Bible verse or stick one on his coffee pot. Do something similar for your siblings as well.
- Ask your family about their lives, and be sincere about it. Try saying, "Tell me about your day," instead of, "How was your day?" Ask your parents what they learned in their small group or at church, and ask your siblings the best and worst parts of their day. Ask how you can pray for each family member.
- Serve your family. Whether you make dinner one night or surprise your mom with flowers, acts of service (big or small) reflect the love of Christ. You will gain joy out of serving your family, and they will appreciate and recognize your selflessness.
- Be honest with your mom, and do not keep secrets from her. Tell your mom what you are going through, and ask her for advice. Moms are usually awesome at providing comfort and listening ears!
- Spend a little quality time with each family member each day. It is not as hard as it sounds – I promise. If the day is coming to a close and you have not spent time with your sibling yet, go to his or her room, and

just sit down and talk for a few minutes. Call your dad on his way home from work or talk with your mom while she cooks dinner. Make time for the people who love you most.

I realize it might be a little awkward to randomly start doing these things. However, **Romans 12:1-2** tells you to **"offer your bodies as a living sacrifice"** and **"do not conform to the pattern of this world."** This means stepping out of your comfort zone to do something that might not be so normal. Coming from someone about to leave her family for college, I encourage you to push through the awkwardness. You do not have much time left to live with your family, so make your impact while you have time left at home. Do your part in building a family focused on Christ. Even though you are young, you can add a little Jesus to your home, so do not waste a second.

further encouragement:
1 Timothy 4:12 ▲ Exodus 20:12 ▲ Psalm 90:12
Matthew 7:24-29 ▲ Romans 12:11 ▲ Matthew 23:11

▲▼▲▼▲▼▲▼▲▼▲▼▲▼▲▼▲▼▲▼▲▼▲▼▲▼▲▼▲▼

serving your family

Matthew 23:11 says, "The greatest among you will be your servant." It sounds a little strange at first to call a servant great. But remember Jesus was the ultimate servant – and you are supposed to follow His example. To show the love of Christ in your family, it is crucial you serve your family. For instance, you could do the dishes each night, randomly make them breakfast, or surprise your siblings with candy. Even small acts of service can bring big smiles! On the following chart, make a list of ways to serve each family member. Let your list serve as a list of goals. Don't just write something down; make it happen!

family member	acts of service

truth or dare

family member	acts of service

broken families

My mom, dad, siblings, and I are not a broken family. We all live together, and we are all Believers. Though we are not perfect, we are not divided by divorce, religion (or lack of religion), addiction, death, or any other major misfortune. However, my mom's side of the family is broken, though I am not going to share the details. In short, my aunt and cousin, both of whom have recently lived with my grandparents, have had some brutal experiences and have made some poor choices. Yet in the brokenness, my grandparents have chosen to love them – because that is all they can do.

I am super close with my Nana, and she often opens up to me about her struggles in holding the family together. She previously took the problem upon herself and wondered why division shadowed her family. She lost hope and even told me she gave up on praying for my aunt. She said she prayed for years only to get no answers.

I cannot give you some magical piece of advice to fix a broken family. I cannot promise that God will answer your prayers exactly the way you want. I just beg you to realize that if you have division within your family, it is not your fault. Whether your family is afflicted by divorce, addiction, or abuse, you did not cause it. Rather, broken families are a result of Satan being in the world. Satan is going to test you and tempt you all he can, and he might do that by disrupting your family. Even so, stay strong in the Lord because He has victory over Satan in the end. In the pain, do not forget who God says He is, and do not forget that He is working for your good even when it does not feel like it (**Romans 8:28**). He is right there beside you in the pain. He does not want to see you distressed, and He is sad for you and with you.

I recently talked with my Nana about her new mindset. I am thankful to say she now understands that she cannot fix the brokenness – only Jesus can. She realized it is not her job to educate, end addictions, or force her family into church. Instead, her new role is to focus on loving my aunt and cousin. While she has always loved them, her ability to love them was shared with her stress and desire to mend everything. Now, lifting everything else up to Jesus, Nana's sole focus is on love. In the anxiety and tears of her family members, her first response is to comfort, pray for, and encourage them – not lecture, complain, or get angry.

Just because Nana loves her family like never before does not mean the wholeness of her family will be restored. I believe her hope lies within **Romans 8:18: "I consider that our present sufferings are not worth comparing with the glory that will be revealed in us."** You might be suffering from a broken family, but have faith that when you choose love in a household full of distress, God's glory will shine through your life. By choosing the path of love, you bring glory to the King. Push through the pain, and live out God's will that you love others and praise Him – even in a world full of division.

further encouragement:
Ephesians 6:10-18 ▲ 1 Peter 5:6-7 ▲ Romans 12:9-16
1 John 4:7 ▲ Matthew 11:28-30 ▲ John 13:34-35

tatum smith

▲▼▲▼▲▼▲▼▲▼▲▼▲▼▲▼▲▼▲▼▲▼▲▼▲▼▲▼▲▼▲▼▲▼

chapter five
DATING

▲▼▲▼▲▼▲▼▲▼▲▼▲▼▲▼▲▼▲▼▲▼▲▼▲▼▲▼▲▼▲▼▲▼

godly dating

Dating is an issue discussed too little in church, and most people, even some truly seeking Jesus, do not understand what it should look like. Godly dating, especially in teenage years, is something I am super passionate about and long for all teens to understand. Because dating did not culturally exist during biblical times, the Bible does not talk specifically about it. However, Believers can draw conclusions from what the Word teaches about marriage to apply to dating. On this one, we are going to jump right into some convicting and life-giving truths.

If you are not okay with being single, then you are not ready to date. You must first be confident in your identity and security in Christ. Not everyone who wants to get married actually does; God does not owe you marriage. Until you can envision yourself being okay without a husband, knowing you will find security and wholeness in Jesus alone, you are not ready to date. If you have this struggle, work on improving your confidence in the Lord's provision, and pray God will give you peace and understanding about being single.

If you are emotionally and spiritually ready to date, maintain high standards. Only date a guy if he will honestly bring you closer to Jesus. Missionary dating, or dating a non-Christian and justifying it by saying you will bring him to Christ, is not biblical. A Godly boyfriend should be as strong in his faith as you are in yours (if not stronger), and you should mutually lead each other closer to the Lord. **Ephesians 5:23 says, "For the husband is the head of the wife as Christ is the**

head of the church, His body, of which He is the Savior." This verse communicates that the guy should lead the girl. Christ leads the church spiritually, so a man should lead a woman spiritually; it is not biblical for a girl to lead a guy closer to Jesus when he is not leading at all. You can definitely provide spiritual encouragement for your boyfriend as long as he is the leader in the relationship – not you.

Do not date a guy if you cannot envision yourself marrying him. I am not saying you must marry him no matter what; I am saying you should date a guy who is compatible with you and marriage material. If he is marriage material, he will lead you closer to Jesus and is obedient to the Word. He has a strong prayer life, studies the Bible daily, and seeks the Lord more than anything else. His actions genuinely reflect his strong faith. He will prioritize his spiritual life over you, and your spiritual life should take priority over him. A marriage material guy will likely have a mentor to hold him accountable in his walk with Jesus and in his relationship with you; he needs to have an older Christian man asking him the tough questions and challenging him to run from sin. He will be involved in a church or even in a small group to ensure accountability. He will have a solid group of Christian friends who bring him even closer to the Lord, and he will give his family higher priority than you. A marriage material guy will always treat you as a treasure in Christ with his words, actions, and thoughts.

It is super important that he pursues you, meaning you should not draw attention to yourself at all. You are like buried treasure, and he should dig to find you; you should not make it too easy for him to pursue you. Not that you should make it overly hard, but you should not be the one texting him first each time and initiating the flirting. That is the guy's job. If he is marriage material, he will pursue you correctly, which means he will do it slowly and patiently to make sure God is indeed leading him toward you. If you have to put yourself out there, dress immodestly, or say or do ungodly things to attract a guy, I assure you he is not marriage material.

Again, your boyfriend should lead you closer to the Lord. He should not be your only source of spiritual growth, but it is awesome if he improves your growth. He should pray for you, and he should take active steps to make Jesus the center of your relationship. Your boyfriend should chase after the cross and encourage you to do the same. Jesus should be the only reason your relationship exists, and you should only be dating if you know without a doubt God wants you to be.

All of this in mind, I am not opposed to dating in high school. I have heard several sermons where high school dating is bashed to no end, and I cannot stand hearing that. Having been involved in a high school relationship that glorifies Jesus, I truly believe high school dating can be beneficial in some rare cases. Nonetheless, it is only acceptable if your parents allow it and if your boyfriend is marriage material.

I realize I have given you an extremely long and picky list of qualities you should look for in a guy and in a relationship. However, you deserve to be picky, as does any Godly girl. Chances are you will not find a guy like this in high school, but it is not impossible. Do not even be worried about trying to find a boyfriend. If you are, that is a sign you are not ready to date. Continue to live your life following Jesus, and God's dating and marriage plan for you will prevail. When it is the right time to date, God will make it plain. He is not trying to confuse you. Wait patiently, and focus on building your relationship with Jesus more than your desire to have a boyfriend.

further encouragement:
Ephesians 5:22-33 ▲ *Mark 10:6-8* ▲ *Ephesians 5:3*
1 Corinthians 13 ▲ *2 Corinthians 6:14* ▲ *Galatians 6:9*

▲▼▲▼▲▼▲▼▲▼▲▼▲▼▲▼▲▼▲▼▲▼▲▼▲▼▲▼▲▼▲▼

boundaries

There are three main types of boundaries in dating relationships: spiritual, emotional, and physical.

The purpose of spiritual boundaries is to make certain you are responsible for your own spiritual walk. If your relationship with Jesus is not your own, then it basically does not exist. Your boyfriend should help your spiritual walk – not be the source of it. He should lead you spiritually – not carry you. Here are some spiritual boundaries I suggest:

- Do not pray with or have deep spiritual conversations with your boyfriend because doing so is too intimate. Avoid conversations about struggles, doubts, or confusions in your spiritual life. Save this for your future husband.
- Do not come to your boyfriend with questions about how to grow spiritually. Ask your accountability

partner or mentors these questions to ensure your boyfriend is not the source of your spiritual life.
- Make sure your boyfriend is not the only reason you go to church. Show up even when he cannot be there.

However, there are practical ways to have Christ at the center of your relationship without crossing spiritual boundaries:
- Exchange prayer requests.
- Memorize Scripture together.
- Study theology or Bible history together (not the application of Scripture to your life; theology and Bible history are less intimate).
- Encourage each other with Scripture.
- Pray for each other daily.

Emotional boundaries are meant to guard your heart like **Proverbs 4:23** encourages. In case it is not God's plan for you to marry your boyfriend, you need to have emotional boundaries so there is limited heartbreak. These boundaries also exist to make sure your future husband is the only man with whom you have a super deep emotional bond. Here are some suggested emotional boundaries:
- Remember only Jesus can fill your heart and give you security. Your boyfriend can never fill this role.
- Do not talk about marriage with your boyfriend because it is not your job to plan your future. God has already done that, and He might have a totally different plan in mind for your relationship. It only

becomes okay to talk about marriage when you are around marriage age and your boyfriend has brought up the subject after much prayer and consideration.
- Do not tell your boyfriend everything you struggle with. He does not need to know all your insecurities and difficulties, but it is fine if you share minor hardships he can be praying for.
- Do not tell him you love him. "I love you" is a commitment – not just a feeling – so save it for your future husband. When you tell a boy you love him, you are giving away a piece of your heart, and only your husband deserves that.
- Do not isolate yourself. Make sure you still spend time with your friends and family and allow your boyfriend to do the same. You and your boyfriend should hang out in groups frequently to balance out your one-on-one dates. An isolated relationship is an unhealthy relationship.

Physical boundaries protect your purity and your relationship with your future husband. The more you save for your husband, the better your marriage will be. God makes it clear in the Bible that He wants Believers to preserve their bodies until marriage, so do not have sex till you are married. Period. **Hebrews 13:4** commands you to keep the marriage bed pure, so there are no exceptions. When you have sex with someone, you automatically give them a special place in your heart. I know girls who have had premarital sex, and many of them have told me they regretfully feel a special connection to the person they lost their virginity to. Sex is the most intimate experience a couple can have, so save it for your husband. No other guy deserves that intimacy with you.

However, if you have already had sex before marriage, you must realize that the Lord makes you new. He cleanses you of that sin as long as you ask for forgiveness and act like you are forgiven. Jesus already paid the penalty, so your shame is gone. It is still possible for you to have Godly marriage because a marriage material man will not judge you for your past mistakes if you seek forgiveness. Start fresh, and do not return to sexual immorality; forgiven people should walk in obedience and freedom from guilt.

While many Christians recognize that premarital sex is sinful, they are often confused on other physical boundaries. Is kissing sinful? What about making out? Surely holding hands is okay!? I have heard these questions from plenty of my friends, and there is no fixed answer. **Ephesians 5:3** says there should be no sexual immorality in you, so if you want to set boundaries against kissing, go for it. I personally believe physical action with your boyfriend becomes sinful when it causes someone in the relationship to lust, or have sexual thoughts. Only kiss your boyfriend if you are positive neither of you will lust. Maybe kissing is not something you or your boyfriend can do without lusting, so set boundaries at the start of your relationship. Here are some thoughts when considering physical boundaries:

- Wait for your first kiss. My first serious boyfriend waited an entire year after we started dating to kiss me, and it helped us take our relationship slowly. I am so

grateful he waited so long, even if I was impatient at the time!
- Think about what you want to save for your husband.
- If it makes you want to go further, do not do it.
- Do not have selfish or impatient physical actions.
- Lengthen your patience. Never lower your standards.

If your Christian boyfriend restrains from doing something physical, it is because he values marriage, fears the Lord, and respects you as His daughter – not because he is not attracted to you. Value a guy who values physical boundaries.

Do not give your boyfriend what only your husband deserves. Set boundaries now so your future marriage will thrive.

further encouragement:
1 Corinthians 6:18-20 ▲ Ephesians 5:3 ▲ Galatians 5:16-19
Matthew 5:27-28 ▲ 1 Thessalonians 4:3-5 ▲ Psalm 119:9

▲▼▲▼▲▼▲▼▲▼▲▼▲▼▲▼▲▼▲▼▲▼▲▼▲▼▲▼▲▼

the godly girlfriend

Just because your boyfriend should be Godly does not mean you have it easy. In fact, you have quite a big role to fulfill as a Godly girlfriend. Here are some tips on how to do so:
- Remember that it is selfish to date your boyfriend simply for fun. Your relationship should exist to glorify God – not just for pleasure or to make you feel good.

- Be the kind of girl you would want your brother to date.
- Pray for your boyfriend and your relationship every day.
- Dress modestly.
- Treat him with respect and recognize that he should put his spiritual walk and family above you.
- Guard his heart, and do not tempt him to sin. Remember that he is your brother in Christ.

If you do not have a boyfriend, there are several ways to prepare yourself to be a Godly girlfriend regardless of how far in the future that might be:

- Be active in your faith; focus on becoming the right person rather than finding the right person.
- Run from the hookup culture. People act like it is okay to hook up with whomever they want whenever they want, but this will only hurt your future relationships, lower your standards, and give you a bad reputation.
- If you are the only one of your friends who has not had her first kiss, realize that is admirable and not embarrassing. Do not kiss a guy just to check it off your bucket list.
- Do not flirt with guys unless one has begun to pursue you in a manner worthy of Christ. Even then, flirt in innocent and respectable ways. Trust me, you do not want to be labeled as a flirt.
- Pray for your future husband. Ask God to prepare your heart to date him and to prepare his heart to date you.

Pray the Lord will make it clear when He wants you in a relationship.
- Regularly read **Proverbs 31**, and strive to be a woman who embodies that passage.
- Pray for your future journey as a girlfriend or wife, if God desires to give you that role.
- Routinely read over the list of qualities you want in a relationship so you are reminded of your standards.

Stick to your morals, and hold yourself to high standards. Be the kind of person you want to attract. A Godly boy is looking for a Godly girl.

further encouragement:
Proverbs 31:10 ▲ Proverbs 31:30 ▲ 1 Peter 3:3-4
Matthew 6:33 ▲ Philippians 2:5 ▲ Galatians 5:16

▲▼▲▼▲▼▲▼▲▼▲▼▲▼▲▼▲▼▲▼▲▼▲▼▲▼▲▼▲▼

modesty

There are two options in the way you dress: clothes that bring glory to God, and clothes that do not. It might sound silly to say clothes can glorify Him, but any modest clothing is pleasing to the Lord. Paul writes in **1 Timothy 2:9-10, "I also want the women to dress modestly, with decency and propriety, adorning themselves, not with elaborate hairstyles or gold or pearls or expensive clothes, but with good deeds, appropriate for women who profess to worship God."** This means you should not bring glory to yourself with how you dress. You should not attract attention by dressing immodestly, and you definitely should not tempt the minds of boys through your clothes. It is normal in today's society to wear shorts that are much too revealing and to show cleavage. It is normal to wear skimpy swimsuits and to send Snapchats in sports bras. But despite how casual dressing like this seems, it is immodest – no matter how you try to justify it.

Girls dress this way to draw attention themselves, whether it is through the eyes of boys or Instagram likes. However, Paul writes that girls should decorate themselves not with clothes (or the lack of), but with God-glorifying deeds. If you dress immodestly, you are not attracting marriage material boys. How you attract a guy is how you will probably lose him, so if you gain his attention through immodesty, he will likely leave you for another immodest girl. Contrarily, if you focus on following Jesus, then you will attract Godly boys who value modesty. And here is a bonus: if you dress appropriately, chances are you will have a better reputation.

Dressing immodestly tempts the minds of boys. When you wear skimpy clothes or post a revealing photo, boys oftentimes cannot help but think inappropriate thoughts simply because that is how they are wired. Think of every male as your brother in Christ. You should guard his heart and protect his mind – not tempt him to have sinful thoughts.

Another modesty issue is the swimsuit. Two-piece swimsuits are the cultural norm even though they look just like bras and underwear. However, I would be a hypocrite if I said not to wear bikinis. If you are going to stick to two-pieces, select modest swimsuits, and throw a shirt on when you are out of the water. Do not post revealing swimsuit pictures on social media; if you do, chances are your motives are a little impure.

Some people might make the personal decision to only wear one-pieces. I have several friends who do this, and I envy their ability to stray from the cultural norm. They see no benefit to wearing bikinis, and they acknowledge that one-piece swimwear is clearly more modest. If you truly believe you can wear a two-piece and still be modest, covering all that needs to be covered and a little more, I can't tell you not to (unless your parents are against it). Otherwise, stick with a one-piece.

Trust me, you want to date boys who value modesty. I have talked to a number of Godly guys who have thanked my friends and me for dressing modestly; they really appreciate and note when you guard their hearts. It does not go unnoticed. Modest is hottest! Don't forget it.

further encouragement:
1 Peter 3:3-4 ▲ *Proverbs 31:30* ▲ *Romans 12:1-2*
Galatians 5:16-18 ▲ *Matthew 5:28* ▲ *1 Thessalonians 5:22*

▲▼▲▼▲▼▲▼▲▼▲▼▲▼▲▼▲▼▲▼▲▼▲▼▲▼▲▼▲▼

dating accountability list

On the following page, make a list of all the qualities you want in a boyfriend or future husband. I encourage you to use suggestions from the "Godly Dating" lesson. Give a copy of your list to a mentor or parent so she can hold you accountable in your dating life. Please, please, please be picky about the qualities you name. Do not settle. Make the list as long as you want.

tatum smith

my dating accountability list:

-
-
-
-
-
-
-
-
-
-
-

dear future husband

Below or on separate paper, write a letter to your future husband. Thank him for being the Godly man he is, and thank him for the ways he has led you and will lead you. This will help hold you accountable in your dating life. Save a copy of the letter, and give it to your husband on your wedding day or soon after.

tatum smith

chapter six
INTERACTIONS

the power of words

Read **James 3**, my favorite passage about the power of words. As a Christian, you are called to live a God-glorifying life in all you do, and this includes your speech. It is easy to encourage people sometimes and to talk about Jesus sometimes and to be optimistic sometimes, but doing so all the time is a whole different story. If people know you follow Jesus, it instantaneously places you on a stage of performance because nonbelievers often look for hypocrisy in the actions and words of Christians. If you claim to be a Believer and then someone hears you gossiping, she will immediately associate that hypocrisy with Christianity. It is your job to honor Jesus with your words because this not only aligns with the Bible, but it also reveals sincerity in your religion. You should want others to view Christians as genuine and dedicated to what they believe – not people whose beliefs do not align with their speech.

Reread **James 3:9-12**. These verses focus on not being hypocritical with words. It makes no sense for someone who claims to be a Christian to go around gossiping or complaining. You cannot praise Jesus and also put others down. The Lord does not just want some of your words, but all of them, and He does not want to be respected with some sentences, but with all of them.

James 3:5 says, "Likewise, the tongue is a small part of the body, but it makes great boasts. Consider what a great forest is set on fire by a small spark." Misspeaking or gossiping once can start an entire "fire," meaning it can cause great trouble. Even one little word that hops off your tongue can change someone's entire view of who you are and who your God is. Your words should stir a fire of encouragement in people's hearts, not a fire of dislike and judgment. This does not mean every sentence you speak must have the word "Jesus" in it. In fact, you can have God-glorifying speech without even mentioning anything about Christianity. Encouraging someone, speaking positive words in negative situations, talking with humility and gentleness, and refusing to gossip all glorify the Kingdom of Heaven. Anything that reflects Jesus and His Word represents your faith well.

In situations when others are gossiping, gently ask them to stop. It can be as simple as, "I don't think we should talk about this right now." Do not call them out on their sinful talk; just silence it. This can be scary, and people might not understand why you do not want to gossip, but stick to your beliefs. If you catch yourself talking bad about someone, stop and apologize to the people you are talking with for gossiping, and then remain quiet throughout the rest of the conversation.

Do not tell your friend when you hear someone gossiping about her unless it is something serious she needs to be aware of. If you tell her about petty gossip, you will only hurt her feelings and encourage her to gossip in revenge. Stand up for your friend, but you do not have to tell her you did so. Sometimes the kindest actions are to be kept secret.

Be mindful of the words you speak in all environments. On sports teams, make sure your every word is encouraging. Harsh comments or tones can cause teammates to dislike you or even your faith. Watch the way you talk around your family because the people who love you most deserve the most loving words. At school, do not be a complainer, but look at your opportunity for education with gratitude. All in all, it truly comes down to thinking before you speak. If it is not positive and does not reflect what you believe, do not say it.

further encouragement:
Ephesians 4:29 ▲ 1 Peter 3:10 ▲ Proverbs 10:19
Proverbs 15:4 ▲ Proverbs 21:23 ▲ Proverbs 31:26

▲▼▲▼▲▼▲▼▲▼▲▼▲▼▲▼▲▼▲▼▲▼▲▼▲▼▲▼▲▼

minimizing conflict

Sometimes, you upset people unintentionally or in the spur of the moment without thinking, such as when you say something hurtful or slip a secret. You have probably been in a situation before in which you hurt someone you care for simply by speaking before thinking.

In **Matthew 22:36-40**, a disciple asks Jesus what the greatest commandment is. Here is His answer: **"Love the Lord your God with all your heart and with all your soul and with all your mind. This is the first and greatest commandment. And the second is like it: 'Love your neighbor as yourself.'"** Jesus longs for you to prioritize Him above everything else, and in doing so, you will learn to value and serve His children. Devote yourself to loving the Lord, and love will consequently overflow in your relationships with others. By striving to put God and His people before yourself, you will hurt fewer people and prevent unnecessary conflict.

To put others before yourself, you cannot tell secrets or

gossip just for attention. You have to quit the one-up game, and you must realize that you are not in competition with your peers. Minimizing conflict sometimes means sucking up your pride and apologizing to someone you have hurt, and it means talking to the girl everyone else makes fun of. God calls you to love other people, to comfort His children, and to think before you speak. When you do so, you will find each day that God becomes greater, and you become less (**John 3:30**).

It is impossible to immediately transition to this humble lifestyle. It takes discipline, prayer, and reminders. Ask an accountability partner or mentor to hold you responsible for putting others before yourself, and pray for the strength, courage, and determination to live out **Matthew 22:36-40**. To be honest, prioritizing the Lord and His people can be embarrassing. It will give you less attention, and it will set you on a path most of your peers will not follow. You must have self-control, and a lot of times it is not fun. In the long run, however, humbling yourself is worth it because it will prevent you from accidentally hurting people you love. Not to mention, people will notice when you put the Lord and others before yourself, and that will attract people to Christianity. When they see you live selflessly yet joyfully, others might realize Jesus is the only explanation.

Another key verse for minimizing conflict is **James 1:19**: **"Everyone should be quick to listen, slow to speak, and slow to become angry."** It is a simple verse, yet it holds a lot of guidance. Have ears ready to listen to anyone; give everyone a voice. You do not necessarily have to agree with what someone is saying, but you must show that you value the person talking to you. Give her your full attention, which means setting down your phone, not interrupting, and not sharing your opinion unless asked. With listening ears, you glorify the Lord and prevent conflict. Next, consider what you are going to say before you speak. Stay silent if your words will not praise Jesus, lift others up, or express grace and gentleness. This will prevent unintentional gossip, criticism, and hypocrisy. Finally, just breathe before you blow up. If someone hurts you, take a step away from the situation. If you can move on or take the path of forgiveness, do so. Just as you let God down over and over again, people will let you down over and over again. Unless an act of hurt is dangerous, it is normally better to let it go. Do not confront someone with an angry attitude, as if you have the right to avenge her, because that will only make the situation worse.

I challenge you to memorize **James 1:19**, as this verse has proved to hold me accountable in my personal experiences. I am confident it will encourage you to use your ears, words, and perspective to minimize conflict.

further encouragement:
Matthew 6:33 ▲ *John 3:30* ▲ *Romans 12:1*
Matthew 23:11 ▲ *Matthew 7:12* ▲ *1 Peter 4:10-11*

▲▼▲▼▲▼▲▼▲▼▲▼▲▼▲▼▲▼▲▼▲▼▲▼▲▼▲▼▲▼

the judgmental stereotype

Christians have a bad reputation for being judgmental. Nonbelievers tend to label Christians as hypocritical, thinking that Believers have strong morals and look down on anyone who does not. I don't blame people who think that either; I have met plenty of judgmental people who also call themselves Christians. It stinks that being judgmental is part of the typical Christian reputation, so how do you change it?

Needless to say, you must stop being judgmental. People are not always going to meet your ethical and biblical standards, and you cannot expect people to live up to your morals. If you are being honest, sometimes you cannot live up to your own standards. If you criticize others for messing up while you remain a sinner, you are being hypocritical. Judgment goes hand in hand with pride. By judging others' actions and words, you are viewing yourself as higher than you are. Ultimately, God is the only judge, so do not waste your time judging others. **James 4:12 says, "There is only one Lawgiver and Judge, the one who is able to save and destroy. But you – who are you to judge your neighbor?"** To stop judging others, start with your words. Really think before you speak, and if your speech will not benefit the Kingdom of Heaven, stay quiet. Then work on your thoughts by praying about it and asking God to cleanse your judgmental heart. It takes discipline, but just remember every time you want to judge someone that you have messed up at some point too (**Romans 3:23**).

Even if you are not judgmental, people will likely give you that label. This might be because you do not drink, do not party, or even because you have a Bible verse in your social media bio. In some people's minds, "Christian" is synonymous with "judgmental." I know you might not have said or done anything drastic to deserve it, but I believe being undeservingly labeled judgmental is part of the persecution Believers face. **2 Timothy 3:12 says, "Everyone who wants to live a Godly life in Christ will be persecuted."** While I am thankful this it is *much* better than alternative forms of persecution, being judgmental is still a hard label to beat. It has hurt my friendships with nonbelievers because they assume I look down upon their actions; they do not invite me to certain events, and they often keep secrets from me because they know I follow Jesus. The stereotype is impossible to avoid, and all my Christian friends would agree. However, Believers can work against this label by *taking it as a challenge.*

It starts with loving people like crazy – loving the people around you so genuinely that they will know you are not judgmental. Respond with gentleness and gratitude when someone confesses a mistake to you, and pray for self-control and humility in your speech. Do not give someone your opinion unless asked, and show no sign of disapproval. You should not affirm your friend's sinful actions, but you should not judge her either. Try being vulnerable with your nonbelieving friends. Let them know you mess up too. I have found the more I share with my nonbelieving friends about what I am struggling with, the more they open up to me.

Dealing with the judgmental Christian reputation is a struggle, but the more you attempt to change it, the more you are doing for the Kingdom. Hang in there, and take it as a challenge.

further encouragement:
James 4:11-12 ▲ Romans 2:1-3 ▲ Romans 14:1
Matthew 7:3-5 ▲ John 15:18 ▲ Matthew 5:10

loving your enemies

There are people in this world who act flat out mean, and there is no getting around it. You will encounter people in all stages of life who do not treat you well, whether it is through their tone, body language, actions, or words. Ever since Adam and Eve ate from the Tree of Knowledge, evil has been instinctive in humans. People are unkind to others when they feel unconfident, insecure, selfish, or hurt, all of which are results of sin in the world. So when dealing with someone who wrongs you, try to hate the sin – not the person. You should not despise God's beloved creations – only the sin within them.

God loves your adversaries you just as much as He loves you like it says in **Romans 2:11: "God does not show favoritism."** Try to imitate His impartiality, and pray for God to give you eyes that view everyone the way He does. I realize it seems impossible to love someone who intentionally wrongs you, but I encourage you to persist: strive to see that person through God's eyes, with love, grace, and forgiveness. Each time you catch yourself thinking negative thoughts about someone, shift your mind to the idea that she was made in God's image and that He loves her deeply.

In Jesus's Sermon on the Mount, He says in **Matthew 5:44, "Love your enemies and pray for those who persecute you."** Loving your enemies is not always a feeling. In fact, you can love someone without liking her. Love is an action, and it is accomplished through praying for your enemies and having Christ-like attitudes and actions around them. Your dislike for someone is not an excuse to shove aside love. It does not justify ungodly thoughts or actions. You are commanded to love others even when they do not love you back.

Love does not seek revenge. **1 Peter 3:9** says, **"Do not repay evil with evil or insult with insult. On the contrary, repay evil with blessing."** Every time someone says or does something to wrong you, do not do it back. Think of your relationship with God: you so often disobey or hurt Him by turning to sin, yet He loves you anyway. He does not hurt you in return, and He does not withhold grace. Try to mimic that love in your relationships with your adversaries. Do not retaliate because retaliation is always an act of selfishness.

Even when you focus on loving your enemies, there is no guarantee they will become kind. However, I guarantee the situation will turn into one that will make you a better follower of Jesus. As you love someone with your mindset and actions, you will grow closer to the Lord by learning to imitate His love.

further encouragement:
Luke 6:27-28 ▲ *Matthew 7:12* ▲ *Proverbs 25:21*
Romans 12:14 ▲ *Luke 6:35* ▲ *Acts 10:34-35*

chapter seven
DIGGING DEEP

drinking

Drinking is an issue you hopefully do not have to deal with in middle school. I used to be in your spot, thinking my close friends would never drink, and I was blind to the truth that as middle school approached its end, so did the innocence of many of my peers. Today, most of my peers drink, and there are only a handful of kids in my grade who have not. Some of my classmates have asked me to drink before, and while I have not given into the temptation, there have been times when I wondered why underage drinking is immoral. Everyone says it's fun, and even some of the nicest people I know do it, so why is it considered sinful?

The Bible instructs Believers not to get drunk. **Ephesians 5:18** makes it clear: **"Do not get drunk on wine, which leads to debauchery*. Instead, be filled with the Spirit."**

*Debauchery means giving into sensual pleasures.

When someone is drunk, she has no control over her mind. **1 Corinthians 10:31** says, **"So whether you eat or drink or whatever you do, do it all for the glory of God."** If you do not have control over your mind, how are you supposed to act for the glory of God? The answer is simple: you cannot. I encourage you to read **Ephesians 5:18** in context. The passage suggests that drunkenness prevents you from being able to make the most of every moment. Maintain control of your mind and flee from intoxication so you can seize every opportunity to love others and follow the Lord.

Many people, including myself, believe it is okay to drink at age 21 or older as long as you avoid intoxication. However, underage drinking is illegal even if you stay sober because the Bible instructs Believers over and over again to respect the government and its laws. For example, **Romans 13:1** says, **"Let everyone be subject to the governing authorities, for there is no authority except that which God has established. The authorities that exist have been established by God."** That means you should respect the government's laws against underage drinking, and in doing so, you will honor the Lord.

Another issue with drinking is association, especially if you are in a position of leadership. Because I lead a student ministry and a Bible study, it would be detrimental to my credibility as a leader if people heard I drink underage; I never want any of my girls in Bible study to doubt my integrity and consistency in what I believe and teach. Yet regardless of whether or not you lead others, remember that association can damage your reputation and cause people to think you are hypocritical in your beliefs, so the most beneficial track is always to stay away from alcohol when you are underage.

All in all, the Bible does not support drinking in middle school and high school. The same goes for doing drugs. Similarly, drugs are illegal (even past age 21 for most drugs), and they hinder your ability to control your own mind and act in a biblical manner. Memorize **Ephesians 5:18** so you will always have a reminder of what the Bible teaches about drunkenness. When you understand why you should not drink underage, you will better withstand temptation, and you will be prepared to answer people who question your choices.

further encouragement:
Ephesians 5:15-20 ▲ *Proverbs 20:1* ▲ *Romans 13:1-5*
Romans 13:11-14 ▲ *1 Peter 2:11-17* ▲ *Hebrews 13:17*
Titus 3:1

▲▼▲▼▲▼▲▼▲▼▲▼▲▼▲▼▲▼▲▼▲▼▲▼▲▼▲▼▲▼

partying

If your peers are not going to wild parties yet, it is only a matter of time before they start. It was around my eighth grade year when crazy parties became popular, even among some of my best friends. You will be shocked and disappointed at some of the decisions your friends make at these parties, and you will probably even be tempted to follow in their footsteps. That is why it is critical to determine what your role is in the world of partying. My best friend and I have taken two very different (yet Godly) paths on this, and while it has been controversial, we have concluded that God has indeed given us different roles when it comes to parties.

Going to parties is not always bad. It is *what happens* at parties that can be sinful, which means it is possible to go to a party and abstain from sin. My best friend decided she wants to go to parties, and she honestly believes God is calling her to do so. Her spiritual life and morals are strong enough that she feels she will not be tempted to drink or partake in sinful actions with boys, friends, or social media at these parties. If she were not confident in this, it would not be acceptable for her to go. Through much prayer and consideration, she believes her role is to go to parties in order to build connections with people she would not get to build otherwise. Her stance is that going to parties shows people she is not judgmental of their actions and that Christians can have fun without drinking. Parties allow her to talk to people she might not normally get to talk to, and this could lead to friendships where she can spread the light of Christ. In addition, going to parties allows her to hold certain friends accountable for their actions (if given permission), as well as drive others home afterward if they are not in a proper state of mind.

I, on the other hand, feel God does not want me to go to parties. Rather, I believe He has called me to be available to people: the Lord does not want me to go to parties so that any of my peers who decide they do not want to go out will have someone to hang out with. For instance, if I have a friend who is struggling with drinking, and she realizes going to a party would be tempting, she will always know she can hang out with me instead. This situation has played out a few times throughout high school, and it has been an awesome way to show some of my friends they do not have to party to have fun. I am not saying I sit at home alone on the weekends waiting for a friend to call me, but I am saying I would cancel any other plans to be there for her.

I also believe going to parties gives people bad associations. Because I hold several leadership positions in my community, going to parties could damage my credibility. Even if I do not make sinful choices, I would not want the teens I lead to associate me with the wild party scene. Going to parties is not worth having someone question my commitment to my beliefs. The same goes for Christians without leadership positions, so if people know you follow Jesus, be cautious of association with parties. Represent your faith well, and give people no reason to doubt your integrity.

I have lost many friends to the party scene. I even had friends who truly chased Jesus and then went to parties, gave up their morals, and brushed aside religion. I personally advise against going to parties unless you are 100% confident God wants you to use parties as a mission zone. Even then, remember that anyone can mess up and fall into temptation – so be on guard.

I encourage you to pray and consider what your role will be in the party world. If you truly believe God is calling you to go to parties like my best friend, then go to some parties, but be sure you will stick to your morals. Always remember to stay on guard. Be cautious that people can misinterpret the sight of you holding a drink, and make sure you never drink out of a cup someone else poured. Even if you want water, pour it yourself because you do not want to risk someone slipping alcohol into your cup. Dress modestly, and be prepared to explain to people why you do not drink.

If you have the slightest worry that going to parties might tempt you, do not go. The damage one party could potentially do to your reputation is not worth it. While grace can always find you in your mistakes, your reputation tends to follow you around, so it is best to prevent sin on the front end. Take the narrow path, and do not go to parties unless your morals are completing unbending.

If you do not feel that God wants you at parties, do not go and know why you made this decision because people will ask. In truth, choosing not to go to parties has been a real struggle for me. It sometimes makes me feel left out and boring, but I know this is really not true, and I know I stand where God wants me. There are other ways to have fun, and I have friends in the same boat as me, so do not think you will be stuck at home every Saturday night if you do not party. There are plenty of other ways to have fun. I am not at home every weekend doing nothing; my friends and I hang out and make memories without going to parties. I would even argue we have far more precious memories than people who spend their every weekend at parties.

Above all, remember **Proverbs 14:12** says, **"There is a way that appears to be right, but in the end it leads to death."** Bending your morals at parties might seem like the cool and acceptable thing to do, but it truly brings you closer to Satan and away from Jesus. It does not lift up the Kingdom. Stand firm in your beliefs, be unwavering in your morals, and know why you stand where you stand.

further encouragement:
Ephesians 5:15-20 ▲ *Romans 12:1-2* ▲ *Titus 2:11-12*
1 John 2:16 ▲ *1 Corinthians 15:58* ▲ *Galatians 1:10*

▲▼▲▼▲▼▲▼▲▼▲▼▲▼▲▼▲▼▲▼▲▼▲▼▲▼▲▼▲▼

cussing

Everyone does it at some point. I am sure you have heard curse words slip out of the mouths of your parents, siblings, or friends, and you have definitely heard foul language on TV shows and movies. Cussing seems to be pretty casual, and it is easy to do. Some of my closest friends and I have all cussed before, though we are not proud of it. Yet despite its normality, cursing does not represent the Kingdom well.

A common excuse people use to justify curse words is that they are just words, nothing more; they are short little words that happen to have bad labels. However, the problem with Christians cussing is connotation, or the feeling/idea that comes along with cuss words. In today's culture, curse words are associated with immorality. When someone who claims to follow Jesus says a cuss word, whoever hears it might automatically develop bad associations for that person. Cursing negatively affects how people view you, so it will likely hurt your ability to show them the light of Jesus. Every word that comes out of your mouth should be for the glory of God, and that rules out curse words.

Ephesians 4:29 says, **"Don't let any unwholesome talk come out of your mouths, but only what is helpful for building others up according to their needs, that it may benefit those who listen."** This verse instructs Believers to only say what is encouraging, which obviously does not include curse words. All of your speech should be uplifting and edifying. It is okay to mess up every once in a while, but that is no excuse to make cussing a habit.

Using God's name in vain is also sinful, although I am guilty of occasionally doing so. The third commandment in the Old Testament says the name of God is holy, or set apart, and in **Matthew 6:9**, the Lord's Prayer says the same. His name should not be thrown around without meaning, so it is sinful to casually say "Oh my God" or any expression of the sort. Do not throw His awesome name around uselessly. The name of the

Lord, the greatest name ever, should only be spoken with sincerity.

Your words should reflect the character of God – not belittle His name. Think before you speak to praise the Kingdom.

further encouragement:
James 3:9-12 ▲ *Philippians 2:9-10* ▲ *Exodus 20:7*
Ephesians 5:3-4 ▲ *Colossians 3:8* ▲ *2 Timothy 2:14-16*

▲▼▲▼▲▼▲▼▲▼▲▼▲▼▲▼▲▼▲▼▲▼▲▼▲▼▲▼▲▼

eating disorders

I have never struggled with an eating disorder, but I know plenty of people who have. They are much more common than you probably think, and they deceitfully take all different forms. From starving themselves to throwing up food to taking laxatives, girls try to minimize the seriousness of eating disorders; they justify their choices or simply keep them hidden.

I understand that eating disorders can be linked to mental health, so if you think your disorder is out of your control, see a trusted adult immediately. Nevertheless, I have many friends who admit they willingly stepped foot on the path of an eating disorder. I want you to realize the magnitude of the simple decision to skip a meal or throw one up. In fact, this is how many of my friend's eating disorders developed. A friend of mine who struggles with anorexia said it started by skipping dinner every few nights, then every night, and then she cut out lunch and breakfast too. It got worse gradually, so it did not seem so bad at the moment. Then it got to the point where she liked feeling hungry.

Many girls fail to realize that eating disorders cause the body serious harm. When you deprive yourself of food, you lack nutrients and can damage your heart, veins, and arteries. If you are tempted to fall into the trap of an eating disorder, I ask you to think of your health as a blessing. Do not jeopardize it. Good health is better than 0% body fat. All throughout the Bible, people ask for healing. From the Psalms to people of Jesus's time, the sorrow of bad health is evident. Good health is a blessing from the Lord that not everyone gets – so do not jeopardize it with an eating disorder. Your body needs nutrients to function correctly, and that means eating food, not just taking vitamins.

If you currently struggle with an eating disorder or are tempted to develop one, read **Matthew 6:25-34**. A friend of mine who struggles with diabulimia uses this passage for comfort and guidance. She says a lot of the pain that comes with eating disorders is the desire to have control, and this passage talks about handing worry to God. Gather the strength to tell a trusted adult or mentor if you are struggling with an eating disorder because these disorders are more than just insecurity. There is hope for you – but only if you pursue it.

Another precious friend of mine struggled with anorexia throughout high school, and this lesson would not be complete without sharing some of her insight. She said starving herself lead to perpetual dizziness and headaches. Even standing up made her feel lightheaded and weak, and she became so accustomed to feeling hungry that she could not differentiate a stomachache and hunger. She found that her eating disorder was a constant in her life; the feeling of being hungry was consistent, and it gave her something to rely on. She definitely agrees it is possible to overcome an eating disorder, but she testifies that its effects will continue to linger in your mind. Nonetheless, if you are struggling with an eating disorder, tell a trusted friend who can be praying for you. To put it simply, her biggest piece of advice was *"Don't start."* If you are burdened by your body image, lift that up to Jesus. Study Scripture on your worth and fulfillment in Christ. Pray like crazy. Stay strong, and do not start skipping meals.

If you do not have an eating disorder but know someone who does, never belittle her struggles. It might not directly affect your daily life, but you must show your friend that you care for her and believe she can overcome it. My friend told me, "The minute someone disregards my eating disorder, I go back to seeing it as no big deal, and it doesn't matter if I don't eat." If someone has confessed an eating disorder to you, pray for her and check in frequently. Remind her it is a big deal, but thankfully she has a big God.

Do not believe the lies that your legs have to be sticks or that tummy rolls are evil. Believe me, legs are fine when they have a little meat on them, and tummies rolls are totally normal. Most girls have them! Society sets an unrealistic standard for bodies, so do not idolize the supermodels or even the swimsuit pictures on Instagram.

further encouragement:
1 Corinthians 10:12-13 ▲ 1 Corinthians 10:31 ▲ Psalm 139:14
1 Samuel 16:7 ▲ 2 Corinthians 12:9-10 ▲ Isaiah 40:29-31

stress

Peace is a word that appears over and over again throughout the Bible, yet it is an abstract concept that is difficult to fully understand. Despite its ambiguity, many people seek peace when they feel stressed out – only to be left in confusion and doubt. **1 Corinthians 14:33 says, "For God is not a god of disorder but of peace."** While this verse sounds comforting, it is hard to believe when stress shadows your circumstances.

Up until recently, I had the idea of peace all wrong. I thought the Lord's peace was something I should naturally feel, and I expected it to magically wrap itself around me when school, sports, or college applications were stressing me out. But when this peace did not miraculously appear, I was confused, and I looked at **1 Corinthians 14:33** in dissatisfaction. I wanted peace to be a savior in stress, and I expected it to bring tranquility to my busy schedule. I thought it was supposed to take away my worry and provide instantaneously comfort.

What I have learned, however, is that God's peace will not take away all the stressful situations in life. Instead, I now believe the explanation of what God's peace truly is lies within the words of **John 16:33** when Jesus says, **"I have told you these things so that in me you may have peace. In this world you will have trouble. But take heart! I have overcome the world."** Jesus spoke these words to His disciples after telling them He was leaving (for Heaven). Obviously, they were stressed out about His departure; how could they follow Jesus if He was not there to lead them? Yet despite their stress, Jesus said they would find peace in Him.

Peace will not totally relieve you of stress because you need hardships to grow closer to the Lord. **John 16:33** basically promises that everyone will have trouble. It does not say you *might* have trouble; it says you *will* have trouble. But take heart. You will find God's peace when you acknowledge that He has overcome the world and its struggles. Your peace comes from knowing Jesus has the victory and that He will crush all of Satan's evil schemes in the end. Your peace comes from knowing you get to spend eternity with Him in Heaven, where there will be no tears, trouble, or stress. Your peace comes from acknowledging that Jesus died for you despite knowing you would never be able to love Him like He loves you. It comes from knowing God holds your future, regardless of your uncertainty. True peace results from seeking God and His triumph over worldly struggles.

Again, this does not mean your stress will go away. Stress can be minimized through good time management and prayer, but it is impossible to completely avoid. When you are stressed out, I encourage you to sit outside for a little bit to journal or talk out loud to God. You will find rest in your quiet time with the Lord, so seek His presence and lean into Him. Let God's peace rule your heart in moments of stress, remembering that whatever you are going through, Jesus has already won the battle.

further encouragement:
Romans 16:20 ▲ *Philippians 4:6-7* ▲ *Colossians 3:15*
1 Peter 5:6-7 ▲ *Psalm 29:11* ▲ *Psalm 34:14*

▲▼▲▼▲▼▲▼▲▼▲▼▲▼▲▼▲▼▲▼▲▼▲▼▲▼▲▼▲▼▲▼

doubt

In some seasons of life, you might question the character of God, and you might doubt His plan, His existence, or His Word. It really boils down to this: you question His goodness. If He is good, His plan, existence, and Word are all legitimate, but if He is not good, He loses credibility. The core of all your doubts is skepticism of His goodness. In moments when your circumstances are trying, confusing, or even heartbreaking, it does not always feel like God is as reliable as His Word proclaims, and there will be moments when you wrestle with Him, even though you are afraid to admit it.

I have had a season when I doubted God's goodness, though I did not want to verbalize it to anyone or even to myself. I have always had a big heart for missions and serving overseas, and at nine years old I developed a dream to go to Africa. This dream turned into reality in the summer of 2017 when I had the opportunity to go to Rwanda, Africa with my youth group. After months and months of fundraising and prayer, my team and I left in July to spend 10 days overseas; my dream was finally becoming reality.

But my dream did not exactly go as planned. I was sick the first half of my trip with gastritis and missed much of my team's ministry. I could not eat, I was vomiting, and I was too miserable to even walk around. I was sick for the following two months after my return and eventually learned I contracted a parasite. If you know me, you know I was devastated. My heart belongs so much to missions, and I believe that is from the Lord, so I was broken when my dream trip turned into a season of pain. I struggled to believe God is good. If He is good, why would He dangle a dream in front of me then yank it away just as I had my fingertips on it? My intentions were to serve and glorify Him, and I felt punished for following His call to Africa.

It would not have been as painful if I had only been sick half of my trip; I could have more easily gotten over that. However, the months of being sick that followed my trip distorted my outlook. It was as if all the preparation leading up to my trip was wasted. While the healthy half of my trip rocked, the following physical, emotional, and spiritual hurt outweighs it in my mind. I wish I would not feel this way, but I continue to reflect on my experience and feel sadness, pain, and doubt. I believe this will heal with time, but I still have a long way to go. I do not wish for this testimony to sound vain or privileged, so I ask you to consider that this experience and my pain was real to me, and it brought serious doubts, although I acknowledge many people go through much worse.

In all honesty, my heart is still healing from being sick during and after my trip to Rwanda. I know God was never working against me, and I know He allowed me to feel doubt so I would eventually hug Him tighter. Nonetheless, I still get overwhelmed when thinking that the same God who allowed a disruption in my dream is the God I call good. But even so, I will continue to speak of His goodness. With the same power through which Paul declared God's goodness even in prison (**Philippians 1**), I will never stop telling people how awesome my God is. That is how I know He is good. If I had abandoned my faith and lost hope that God is who He claims to be, He would not be good. The fact that the Lord so graciously allows me to follow Him, that He allows me to know deep down that all of this is real, that is my proof He is good. The fact I could never turn away from the Kingdom, that I could never deny Him, that is my proof. If God was bad, He would let me abandon Him. He would let me run away from what He promises, and He would let me disastrously become my own god. But for some reason, I know I could never. Even if I tried to run from the Lord, I know I would return. That is how I know He is good.

If you are in a season of difficulty and have doubts about God's goodness, know it is okay. You are small, God is big, and you will not always understand His ways. Meditate on **Isaiah 55:8-9**, and embrace that doubt. Wrestle with it. One way to do this is to journal your ups and downs of the past season; write down all of the awesome experiences and all of the not so awesome experiences. I did this exercise at the end of 2017, and I found myself astonished at how I could have possibly questioned God's goodness. The same season in which He allowed misfortune, He also filled with some of the biggest blessings, though I wish to keep my personal examples to myself. I encourage you to do the same, because the more you verbalize your blessings from the Lord, the more you will see His goodness. The more you seek His faithfulness, looking for it daily, the more you will recognize it. Confusion or pain may still be there, but His goodness outweighs it every time if you allow it. Healing will come with time and waiting. Use that season of waiting to highlight the blessings in your life, and healing will only come faster.

I realize this is a short answer and probably the one you were expecting. However, doubting the Lord is something that looks different for everyone in every season. Thus, I encourage you to chat with a mentor or friend about your doubts and pray for God to give you a believing heart.

further encouragement:
Psalm 23 ▲ Psalm 71:15 ▲ Philippians 4:19
Psalm 27:13-14 ▲ Romans 8:28 ▲ 2 Thessalonians 3:3-5

tatum smith

chapter eight
DISCIPLESHIP

accountability

You are not called to grow closer to Jesus all on your own. **Hebrews 10:24 says, "Let us consider how we may spur one another on toward love and good deeds."** Life is tough, and it is easy to get distracted from Jesus in times of craziness, confusion, anger, or stress. That is why everyone needs accountability. A church term often used is "accountability partner." An accountability partner is a person (oftentimes a close friend) who holds you responsible for your actions and spiritual walk, in whatever form that takes. Accountability goes two ways (unless it is coming from a mentor), so you would ideally hold your partner responsible for her spiritual walk as well.

Selecting a good accountability partner is so important for the future of your walk with Jesus. You want your partner to be a girl around your age so you will have better empathy for each other. It needs to be someone you are comfortable opening up to about things you might not discuss with others, such as what has been hard in your spiritual life or what you are struggling with. Most importantly, you want an accountability partner who will truly encourage you to grow closer to the Lord and will help you overcome sin struggles and hard times. After spending time in prayer and carefully considering who would be a great accountability partner, ask that friend if she wants to hold you responsible in your spiritual walk, and ask if she wants you to do the same for her. Do not be intimidated because accountability is nothing fancy. Realize that this relationship does not have to be scheduled or follow a set of rules. An accountability relationship can start simply by having honest and genuine conversations. Just talk about life, and do not be afraid to get deep, and you will be off to an awesome start.

A great accountability partner consistently prays for her partner, acknowledging that prayer will strengthen their bond and solidify their commitment to bring each other closer to Jesus. She is always gentle and never becomes annoyed or frustrated when her partner shares what she is going through. She understands that even if her friend's struggle seems silly to her, it is real to her friend. A great accountability partner is also trustworthy. She does not tell others about what her partner has shared unless it is dangerous and an adult needs to know. She makes time for her partner and always has listening ears. She points her friend back to the Bible, and she hangs out with her regularly to discuss life and where she stands with Jesus. She challenges her friend to grow closer to Him and to overcome her sin struggles. She asks her partner what areas she can grow in, and she shares her own areas of potential growth. She calls her friend out in a gentle and loving manner when she sees her sinning; she is not judgmental, and her intentions are not to elevate herself. She encourages and uplifts and prays. She brings her partner back to truth and reminds her that her primary goal on this planet is to grow closer to and glorify Jesus. I encourage you to find this great accountability partner and to be this great accountability partner.

It is important to note that being held accountable can be difficult. It is not fun when someone tells you that you are messing up or drifting away from the Lord. It can be embarrassing and mess with your pride, but ultimately, it is beneficial for you to accept correction. Without a partner to warn you that you are straying from Jesus, you might not even notice you are doing so. Other people are usually better at recognizing your faults than you are! **Proverbs 19:20** says, **"Listen to advice and accept discipline, and at the end you will be counted among the wise."** Scripture makes it clear that accountability makes you wiser in the long run, even if it makes you angry in a moment.

Start searching your heart now and looking for areas you need to mature in or sin struggles you need to overcome. There is always a way to grow. Start praying for your accountability partner, even if you do not know who she is yet. Ask God to reveal one to you, and He will not leave you shortchanged. I challenge you to make your relationship with your accountability partner strong and nourishing, centered on and running toward Jesus.

further encouragement:
1 Thessalonians 5:11 ▲ *James 5:16* ▲ *Proverbs 27:17*
Galatians 6:1-5 ▲ *Hebrews 10:24-25* ▲ *Hebrews 12:11*

▲▼▲▼▲▼▲▼▲▼▲▼▲▼▲▼▲▼▲▼▲▼▲▼▲▼▲▼▲▼

mentorships

A mentor is different than an accountability partner in that she is older and more experienced, so she can provide wise one-way accountability. An awesome example of mentorship in the Bible is the relationship between Paul and Timothy. Paul served as Timothy's mentor and wrote him letters to encourage him in his faith. He provided biblical encouragement and support for Timothy, and I believe every Christian should find a mentor to do the same for her. To learn more about how Paul mentored Timothy, I encourage you to read **1 Timothy** and **2 Timothy** and observe the encouragement, accountability, and guidance Paul provided. He also mentored Titus, so the book of **Titus** is another great example of mentorship.

Some mentorships come naturally. For instance, if you grew up in the church, your mom or small group leaders might be built-in mentors in your life. Other mentors, however, you might have to seek out yourself, especially when you go off to college or move to a different city. To select a mentor, look for a person whose character and faith you want to imitate. You want her to be fun, strong in her spiritual life, and eager to show others the love of Jesus. You should feel comfortable around her and be willing to open up to her about your sin. It is perfectly fine, even beneficial, to have more than one mentor as long as you are not spreading yourself too thin. When you have found an older woman to lead you, ask her if she would be willing to mentor you. It sounds a little awkward, but a casual way to start is to ask her to chat over coffee or ice cream.

Mentorship does not have to be anything fancy; your mentor does not have to write out Bible studies for you or take you to church. Oftentimes, talking with a mentor is simply talking about life. Just update your mentor on your current season, and she will do her best to provide any advice or encouragement you need. There is one catch: you have to be totally open with her. If you want your mentor to care for, pray for, encourage, and love every part of you, you must tell her everything. If you hide something because you think it is too sinful, dirty, or unlovable, distance will grow in your relationship. If she is a true mentor, she will love you regardless of your sin. Nonetheless, it is part of her job to ask you tough questions. She is hopefully going to ask what has been hard for you or what you are struggling with, so be prepared to give an honest answer. The more truthful and vulnerable you are with her, the more fulfilling and beneficial your relationship will be.

Just because mentorship is one-way accountability does not mean it is one-way everything. You are responsible for keeping in touch with, opening up to, and making time for your mentor. You must answer her texts and calls, and you should take her advice. Pray for your mentor, and be thankful she willingly gives her time and energy to invest in you and your faith.

If you do not currently have a mentor, pray for the Lord to guide you to one. Mentorships will sharpen your character and faith, so start seeking a woman who can lead you now.

further encouragement:
Proverbs 15:22 ▲ *2 Timothy 2:2* ▲ *Titus 2:3-8*
Proverbs 9:9 ▲ *Hebrews 13:7* ▲ *Proverbs 22:6*

▲▼▲▼▲▼▲▼▲▼▲▼▲▼▲▼▲▼▲▼▲▼▲▼▲▼

scripture memory

"**For the word of God is alive and active. Sharper than any double-edged sword, it penetrates even to dividing soul and spirit, joints and marrow; it judges the thoughts and attitudes of the heart.**" Those are the powerful words of **Hebrews 4:12**. Alive and active – that means what the Bible says is powerful and applicable today. Sharper than a sword – that means the Bible is your best weapon in fighting Satan. Judges the mind and heart – that means the Bible teaches and convicts you. Everything **Hebrews 4:12** says the Word does is super beneficial…so why don't you memorize what it says? The Bible is literally the most important book on the whole entire planet because it is the only physical form of communication Believers have from God. It provides guidance, encouragement, and truth, so it is important to memorize what it says. You obviously do not have to memorize the whole entire Bible, but I do challenge you to memorize as much of it as you can.

Scripture memory is important because it helps you make disciples. Every follower of Jesus is called to teach others about Him, and you need to memorize Scripture to help you do this. When you are telling someone about your beliefs, you should be able to back up what you say with Bible verses; you need to prove that your beliefs are biblically founded. By memorizing Scripture, you will also remember why you believe what you believe, and this will give you a firm foundation for your morals. The verses used throughout this book are great ones to memorize because they are to-the-point and easily applicable to life. You will even be able to share them with people who ask you why you act a certain way or do not partake in certain actions.

In addition, I encourage you to memorize encouraging Bible verses. When you have comforting verses memorized, you can think back to them on bad days or tough seasons, and you can also use them to lift up others. It is important to share encouraging Bible verses with people you disciple to remind them of your commitment to and love for them.

Memorizing Scripture is not easy. Rather, it is easy to forget about. A practical way to ensure you are consistently memorizing Scripture is to set a reminder on your phone for every two weeks that says "scripture memory." Next, I suggest writing the verse you are currently memorizing in a place where you frequently see it, such as in your planner or setting it as your phone background. Switch up the location every once in awhile to make sure you do not begin to overlook it. Say the Bible verse aloud to yourself a couple times a day, and try memorizing it with a friend, family member, or mentor to gain some extra encouragement and accountability. My favorite way to memorize a verse is to write the first letter of each word on my hand or arm. This strategy will help guide you in memorizing the verse without giving it away. I have also found a little bonus to this technique: people will ask what the random letters written on you are, meaning you will have the chance to tell them about Scripture. Lastly, I suggest you keep a list of every Bible verse you have memorized so you can periodically quiz yourself to make sure they remain in your long-term memory.

Scripture memory will remind you how to live as a follower of Jesus and will equip you to share your beliefs with others. Keeping a library of Bible verses in your mind ultimately helps you and the people around you, so do not overlook the opportunity to memorize tidbits of the most perfect book on earth.

further encouragement:
2 Timothy 3:16-17 ▲ *Psalm 119:11* ▲ *Joshua 1:8*
Colossians 3:16 ▲ *Matthew 4:4* ▲ *Psalm 37:30-31*

▲▼▲▼▲▼▲▼▲▼▲▼▲▼▲▼▲▼▲▼▲▼▲▼▲▼▲▼

multiplication

Multiplication of disciples is based off the verse 2 Timothy 2:2 when Paul writes to Timothy, "**And the things you have heard me say in the presence of many witnesses entrust to reliable people who will also be qualified to teach others.**" Basically, Paul led Timothy and Titus so they would eventually lead others. By repeating this process, the total number of Believers begins to grow exponentially. Here is a picture of this idea:

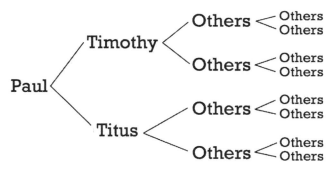

Believers make disciples to make disciples to make disciples. I hope throughout this book I have helped you grow closer to Jesus and have revealed truths to you about who He is and how He has called you to live. However, I have not shared my biblical understanding with you so you can keep it to yourself. Just as my mentors taught me more about Jesus, I hope I have taught you more about Him so you can teach others.

Making disciples will look different for every single person reading this. Some of you might begin to mentor your little sister, while others might mentor girls at school. Some might get involved in a Christian ministry or even start a Bible study. I have friends who pray with people while volunteering at homeless shelters. Some of my friends teach kids about Jesus in Sunday school, and some have started Bible studies similar to mine. A group of peers helps me run a student ministry at my school, and others have blogs about what the Lord is doing in their lives. The opportunities to make disciples are endless, and my peers have instilled great confidence within me that our generation can increasingly expand the Kingdom.

No matter what it looks like for you, make sure you do your part in discipleship and multiplication. Never think you have to reach a certain standard to be equipped to lead others. If you follow Jesus and have access to a Bible, no matter how much you know, you are ready to go. Believe me, when I started my Bible study, I had no idea how I was going to make it happen, but through prayer and submission to the Lord, He moved. I am confident He will do the same for you. After praying about how God will use you to make disciples, talk with a mentor about how you can make it happen.

This is the truth I leave you with, and now it is your job to determine what you are going to do with it. The process of discipleship is not complete until you have made disciples yourself. Make disciples who make disciples who make disciples.

truth or dare

further encouragement:
Matthew 28:18-20 ▲ *2 Timothy 3:16-17* ▲ *Colossians 3:16*
Acts 2:42-47 ▲ *Acts 6:7* ▲ *Hebrews 4:12*

▲▼▲▼▲▼▲▼▲▼▲▼▲▼▲▼▲▼▲▼▲▼▲▼▲▼▲▼▲▼▲▼

truth or dare

about the author

Tatum Smith is a high school student in Little Rock, Arkansas, where she lives with her parents and two siblings. While leading ten middle school girls in Bible study, Tatum wrote *Truth or Dare* with the intention of preparing her study group to face high school in firm faith. Tatum also spends her time running a student ministry, coaching Upward Soccer, and fundraising for an opportunity center in Guatemala City.

Made in the USA
Lexington, KY
24 April 2018